Habits of Being

Habits of Being:

Artifacts from the Classroom Guild

By Kimberly Bredberg

blackbird & company
EDUCATIONAL PRESS

Blackbird & Company Educational Press, Los Angeles, California

Library of Congress Control Number: 2011932974

ISBN 978-1-937200-00-8 (paperback)

Executive Editor: Sara Evans

Associate Editors: Sherry Kidd, Christian Nichols

Book Design: Brian Lane

blackbirdandcompany.com

Printed in the United States of America

Currahee, we stand alone together.

•

•

for Hannah, for Taylor, for Liam, for Søren—I delight as your individuality blooms; my heart... yesternight and tomorrows ever after

and for Willie, because when it's been what it should have been, I will follow you into the dark where the LOST will gather in a sideways room

contents

Be what God made you to be
and you will set the world on fire.

—Catherine of Siena

DEAR READER,

As a child, I sensed something missing in the classroom and I found this something much more disturbing than the bully on the playground. I was spending my days participating in plentiful nothing.

I sensed my individuality shrinking.

Back then I could not give voice to the stirring, but if I could it might have sounded something like this: "Something has to be done about the lack of creative opportunity at my school." A desire for justice clamored in my elementary school mind like a tap tap tapping on my shoulder. For years and years the tapping ended with a, "But who am I?" decrescendo.

This doubting made the task of responding to that tap tap tap slow going.

When I was in the 2nd grade, several of my friends were called out of class for a visit to the principal's office. The good news is they came back one at a time with a smile on their face. It seems they were crowned MGM students—Mentally Gifted Minors.

On one hand, I was happy for my friends. On the other hand, I was conflicted for those of us left behind. Even in the second grade, I believed that the pool of genius was larger than the powers-that-be were able to recognize.

When, in middle school, the Renaissance was introduced, I raised my voice in dissent to the teacher who communicated that genius is rare, that the Renaissance was a pocket of history rich with the stuff of genius. I simply could not accept her view.

"Leonardo and Michaelangelo," I declared, "were apprenticed. We're not." I saw the teacher's eyes roll, received a pat-on-the-back response, and the lesson moved on through the checklist of standards allotted for that day.

I spent the rest of that 5th period history class mourning lost potential. What if each and every one of us was apprenticed?

Apprentices are mentored in a guild. Researching the definition of the word guild, I discover that the term can be used to define ecosystems in nature, giving us the perfect illustration of a community thriving on interdependence.

So here I am, all grown up, still believing the potential that was nurtured through Leonardo and Michelangelo's guild apprenticeships can be realized in all of education. After many years of being an educator, I am still concerned, "When it comes to the education of our children, something has to be done about the lack of creative opportunity."

My friends are people just like you. Some of my friends send their children to public school, some to private school. Some of my friends have chosen to homeschool. My hope is that the message of this book will infuse all domains of education choice.

I engage every student apprentice who crosses my path in activities that stir the development of Creative Critical

Thinking. And I delight catching glimpses of the individual genius that transpires. After years of empowering parents with, “Yes you can!” this message is for you.

For a dozen years I have partnered with like-minded parents who dare to step into my classroom guild, dare to allow a measure of the creative chaos that unveils the individuality of their children. Some days ended with scribbles on bathroom walls, tempera stains on the carpet, chipped teacups, and Legos strewn from one end of the house to the other. Some days ended in tears. But most days, I wanted to stand on that proverbial soap box and beg people to come to my guild and be inspired.

Childhood is precious.

Most days I left the guild with something profound, shaping my own individuality.

You may read this offering and think, “Yeah, right.”

Know that the philosophy I am presenting was born of day in, day out. I want to assure you there were endless conversations to combat doubt, “Am I doing the right thing here?” At times I thought I would crumble with the weight of spontaneous and often chaotic guild activities.

But Hindsight brings clarity.

I can see how it might be easy to become overwhelmed by what seems a litany of creative accomplishment. Be assured, the stories here are not of children or parents who are more exceptional than your children or you. The stories here are a result of artful education and the curiosities of days and hours.

Don't be overwhelmed!

The sad truth is, I have had many people tell me that my children—even the students in my guild—posses rare genius, as if my little program is some sort of magnet.

Not true.

All children have latent genius; yours included.

The Guild Method is a longitudinal approach in which the student apprentice is taught that learning is a steady progression over time that allows deep Habits of Being to develop.

Habits of Being make us who we are.

As you wander with me through the pages of this book, remember to read between the lines. Alongside the guild activities, designed to promote a passion for discovery and learning, there is ample room for hours of play. Play is not frivolous; it is an essential ingredient of childhood, is the work where the child begins to discover the essence of imagination and to explore the creative impulse.

Above all else, I hope that each of you will read this work eyes wide open. I believe in the potential of your child and I believe in your potential to awaken the slumbering genius.

—Kimberly

Ingredients of the Guild Method

the classroom guild

Renaissance is literally a revival.

The Guild is the ecosystem that drives that revival.

If ecology is the study of living organisms and their relationship with the environment, and if we are to transfer this model to the field of education, then we must begin by embracing the diversity of the living organisms we are trying to promote—the individuality of the child.

Ecology is not to be taken for granted.

A delicate balance must be maintained for an ecosystem to be preserved. Inside the classroom guild, student apprentices are encouraged to actively respond to their environment. The Guild Method has been forged to develop Critical Creative Thinking in children. This is not to say that the Guild Method is limited to artistic pursuits. Quite the contrary, creativity is a process of thought. Developing creative literacy is to move beyond the base skills that allow us to read and write. Creative literacy is achieved as student apprentices begin to imagine possibility and to delight in the work of pursuing knowledge.

We need to keep in mind that the heart and soul of the child is precious. In the classroom guild, protection and promotion of individuality is the wonderful work that leads to active learning and soul satisfaction. We all know that there is a mountain to climb before the intrinsic rewards from the work of learning kick in. And we know that there is much to threaten the ecosystem of the Guild. Procrastination and perfectionism are common pestilence. But even these threats will be overcome as the apprentice commits to a longitudinal journey towards mastery.

the artful educator

Harkening back to the Renaissance guild mentorship, the goal of the Artful Educator is to help children cultivate their natural strengths by encouraging them to work through their weaknesses. Walking alongside children as they press into the important work of becoming educated leads to individual excellence.

Artful Educators are mentors who serve as both a guide and collaborator working alongside the child. Recognizing that each child possesses the potential for genius, the mentor coaxes children to discover the potential of their individuality. By presenting authentic tasks and emphasizing discovery, the Artful Educator's goal is to support the curiosity of each child apprentice and to spark the creative impulse, thus setting the art of learning into motion.

The Artful Educator recognizes the extraordinary in each child; believes that children are capable of self-directed learning.

The Artful Educator adapts to the brilliance of the young mind and inspires the student toward purposeful action.

The Artful Educator provides scope for meaningful exploration.

The Artful Educator whets curiosity; encourages depth and breadth in learning.

The Artful Educator is a sailing instructor...

> I'm not afraid of storms, for I'm learning how to sail my ship.
>
> *–Louisa May Alcott*

the child apprentice

Each child has been endowed with genius.

Curiosity is the motivator that sparks innovation. Curiosity invites us to imagine possibility.

Under the capable and nurturing mentorship of the Artful Educator, the child apprentice will learn to analyze, interpret, and reflect. Children will embrace and engage in the work of becoming educated as they are encouraged to enjoy the pursuit of knowledge and skill. Inside the Classroom Guild, apprentices will engage over time in a broad scope of meaningful exploration in diverse subject areas and acquire a personal academic of responsibility.

Learning is an unruly algorithm, a one-step-at-a-time journey with unexpected side strolls. Excellence is achieved as the student apprentice learns to value his or her creative impulse and is provided opportunities to respond to that impulse.

To be exceptional requires sincere practice that is seated in the heart. Caring about work makes work meaningful. In the same way the musician practices scales and the artist draws lines, textures and shapes, The Guild Method helps children discover and develop the skills that allow them to successfully press into and accomplish long-term meaningful work. It's true that practice makes perfect. But not all practice develops meaningful outcomes. The right kinds of practice over time build habits of being and Habits of Being make us who we are.

PREAMBLE
on the nature of going out my front door

> There is nothing like looking, if you want to find something. You certainly usually find something, if you look, but it is not always quite the something you were after.
>
> –*J.R.R. Tolkien*

I have a collection of tincture bottles displayed on a glass pedestal in my living room that I use to vase single wildflowers. So the flowers are not exactly wild, but I can dream, can't I?

Sometimes this city girl has to settle for whatever delicate variety Trader Joe's has stocked in the produce section. At any rate, I enjoy creating installations near the dining table, "My choir of nature," I remind the family.

The very act of clipping the flowers, getting the height just right so each little head will be visible, adding just enough water to the bottles and drying the glass so that refraction of the stem in water is accentuated, is ikebana to be sure.

Once upon a time, well into spring, I realized that my little tincture bottles were flowerless. I stepped out my back door, heeded Tolkien's warning, plopped myself on the driveway to count the weeds with the very same words in mind.

My contemplative journey was interrupted by my smallest son's voice.

"What are you doing mom?"

"Counting dandelion crowns."

"What do you mean?" He sat down beside me.

"Do you see those yellow flowers?"

"Yes."

"Those are dandelions. I made a crown of them for Hannah when she was your age."

"How?"

"I gathered a bunch." I proceeded to pick a couple of flowers to demonstrate. Took my fingernail to stem, made a small slit and slipped one flower's stem through the slit of the other. "I did this with a bunch of flowers until my chain was long enough for a crown." I still remember twisting the last stem around the first, "Do you know what your sister said when I placed the crown on her head?"

"No."

"I'm the queen of the *daisylions*!"

"*Daisylions*? That's funny." Another nod. "But aren't dandelions those flowers we blow into the sky?"

"Yes, but they are golden flower heads before they are puffy seed heads." I could see my son's eyes widen, reflecting the marvel I felt upon discovering this wonder of creation.

"Do you want to gather some dandelion's with me for the tincture bottles?"

"Sure."

The next day my son came racing into the house. "Mom! Come here! You have got to see this, hurry. Come on!"

I followed Søren to the front yard.

"This one was a flower yesterday. Remember?"

"Yes, I do! I have read that the flowers transform into seed overnight."

"We saw, mom!"

"Those tiny seeds will parachute afar. They say dandelion seeds carry dreams on the wind."

Later that day I was setting the table for dinner, and the dandelion choir echoing from tincture bottles assembled on the glass pedestal reminded me of another mystery.

My in-laws have an acrylic cube that, to me, is much more than part of the décor. The pesky little object taunts me. "How did this happen?" I have asked myself this for more than twenty-five years. Trapped inside that cube is a perfect dandelion seed head, its individuality thwarted. I want to huff and puff and release the potential. I wonder where those seeds would have blown, what they might have become. But I'll never know because they are locked inside a solid acrylic cube.

The dandelion cube

Dandelions are dogged little plants. I tug at the brittle taproot, twist twist twist to stop the weed from propagating. Thing is, it will regenerate. The weed always wins. Like the child, it thrives in diverse settings with a single purpose: to cast its talent to life.

I can't help but wonder why we encase children in an acrylic mode of education where everyone is taught the same thing on the same day at the expense of cultivating individuality? Can't help but wonder why we tug at the taproot, twist twist twist potential from soil?

A child is not a weed to be tamed.

Childhood is wildly toothsome, full of potential.

ONE / *The Sky is Falling*

The sound you are about to hear is not the cluck of Henny Penny, is not a response to an acorn fallen from a tree. Looking out at the landscape of education in America, I can't help but cry, "The sky *is* falling."

I receive calls on a regular basis from parents deeply concerned by apathetic, and often dangerous, behavioral tendencies in their uninspired fifteen-or-so-year-olds.

My heart breaks each and every time.

I recognize that the solution to this dilemma is simultaneously simple and complex. Change involves a singular choice followed by a complex choreography that can only be accomplished longitudinally, one step at a time.

Choreography? As an example, let's begin with books.

More than one parent has asked me, "What does learning to read and write have to do with promoting individuality?"

Great stories are chock-a-block with possibility.

Possibility has the potential to spark curiosity.

Curiosity leads to imagination.

Imagination fuels dreams.

Over the years I have mentored countless high school students whose GPA does not reflect the individual's potential. In such cases, I begin as I always do, by handing the student a book. Stimulating the heart, the mind, and the soul is essential to a full academic experience.

Great stories do not merely contain the potential to be instructive, but to be experiential. For those who know how to use them, books will spark curiosity, evoke imagination, and foster critical creative thinking. Because the intellectual, emotional, and spiritual components of a story are insepa rable,a single story can profoundly impact an individual.

Great stories encourage us to revel in the beauty of creation, coax us to embrace heroism, fight injustice, may inspire us to love our neighbor as ourselves.

Great stories encourage us to persevere in the com plex tasks we encounter while reaching for life's potential.

But how do we inspire our students to read?

Illiteracy is becoming much more than an inability to decipher letters on a page.

Illiteracy has become a lack of desire to decipher the world at large.

What is lost when our children are so discouraged by stand ardized tasks that they loose heart and don't care about the important work of mining for the academic gold?

The answer is queuing in my mind's eye. Their nameless faces cluster across the desk from me pleading, "Help!" These are individuals whose creativity, ranging from scientific, to artistic, to mathematical, to interpersonal, is being left unattended.

School has failed them.

These are the students who were once small children with big dreams — the sculptor, the future President of the United States, the poet, the archeologist, the prima ballerina, the architect — only now they are closer to grown up and scared by their withering dreams, terrified of the work force.

I take them by the hand, stand with them at the first page of a book.

I remind them that it is never too late, "In this particu lar story, as seventh grade comes to a close, Allegra Leah Shapiro has been selected as a finalist in a prestigious violin competition and this stirs up all sorts of inner conflict..."

Why does summer have to be so hectic?

What does it mean to be half Jew and half gentile?

Why is soprano, Diedre, crying?

How can I be a twelve-year-old violinist and have time to be a friend?

Why is my brother so annoying?

How has Mr. Trouble lost his song?

What is this gift from Bubbe Raisa?

And what of this great-grandmother I've been named after?

Will I be able to dig deep enough for Mozart?

Can I undo what has been done?

I believe with all of my heart that this character, Allegra, might be able to inform these uninspired fifteen-or so-year-olds. I believe that (if they dare to read between the lines) they will hear the whisper, "You are not alone."

"*The Mozart Season*," I tell them, "is a quiet story, one filled with resounding music that just might change your life." I leave it there, hand them the book and ask them, well, okay, *require* them, to read a bit so we can discuss the story in a week.

I'm always hopeful, but when a week has passed, I know they will still be at the starting blocks. This race is never a sprint.

"So have you completed the reading?"

"Well, no, not really, I mean, well..."

"This was required reading."

"I just really don't get it."

Now I'm sure this is not about the words on the page. These are students who know how to read, thing is, they have no idea how to be inspired by a story, have no idea how to embrace the universal truths — the archetypes embedded in books — and apply them to their lives. They have no idea how to animate a character like Allegra.

So I read the opening paragraph of the first chapter:

> In Mr. Kaplan's studio is a needlepoint pillow, on a chair. On one side of it is a violin. The other side says, *A teacher is someone who makes you believe you can do it.* Somebody who took lessons from him a long time ago made it. When I was little, I couldn't read it clearly because needlepoint letters have odd shapes.[1]

"Seems to me Virginia Euwer Wol is using pretty plain language."

"Um, I don't know," they reply.

"Has anyone ever told you that a great story is a mentor?"

They are about to roll their eyes, but miraculously trust me instead, "What?"

"If we dig deep enough into the heart of a story, dig to its very core, I believe we will always discover a treasure to inform our own life. A good mentor leads us by the hand on an exploration of discovery that will make us a richer person."

"But my mind wanders when I read."

"Mine too."

"Really?"

"Yes. I've worked to slow down, worked to build habits that help me ponder words, phrases, passages—their peculiar shape, sound and meaning. And these habits I've built, have enabled me to value reading. I've learned to love stories because I know stories will enrich my individuality. I know you can too. I want to help you do the same because your individuality matters."

They beam, but only for an instant. "Don't be overwhelmed, I'm going to walk with you, one step this way then one step that way."

Long after we completed our close reading of The Mozart Season, I gather the apprentices in the classroom guild

—primary, elementary, middle and high school together—to congratulate our young writers and artists who were recognized by Scholastic Alliance for Young Artists & Writers this year, along with students who had work published in literary journals.

As I am handing out the awards, it dawns on me that four of the award winning projects began with the writers and artists responding to The Mozart Season and blossomed into something imaginatively original.

The Wind and the Rain

(http://bit.ly/Wind-and-Rain)

Curiosity ignites critical creative thought.

Critical creative thought is the door to originality.

Some children have not been taught to value their ima-gin-ation. Some children have not established a routine of critical creative thinking. These are the children who have never learned to read deeply, These are the creative illit erates.

So I scan the room for those left behind to remind them with my very own eyes, You don't have to be a concert violinist to relate to Allegra. Her story has much to offer if you dare to do the important work of building a habit of being.

A friend of mine has a daughter who is the same age as my eldest son. We meet regularly for coffee, compare notes. Recently we gathered, a steamy mocha nestled in my palms, my friend's weariness a neatly packaged time bomb.

"I'm worried."

"Clearly."

"Grades have slipped, but it's worse. Her teachers are threatening expulsion."

"What do you think?"

"Well, you know she's always struggled, but this is something else. She's restless and brutally rebellious. I feel like our relationship has been reduced to an incessant NO. She informed us in no uncertain terms that she hates school."

In the next breath my friend tells me that her daughter threatened to report them—her parents—to social services if they continued to bug her about grades, told them she wants to be emancipated from their *abuse*.

My friend's eyes pooled, so did mine.

"She's lost sight of her purpose."

"When we were notified that she has a mountain of unexcused absences and is failing four classes, we took away her cell phone. And then two days later she snatched the phone from my purse, slipped it into her backpack, and went on with her life. I called the phone company and had the service suspended."

"Did it do the trick?"

"Not really. I am tired and worried about high school next year. I want to make a change."

"You know that's baited, right?"

"Go ahead."

"Transitioning from middle school to high school is an opportunity. After all these years, you know I can help if you let me."

"It's been different for your children, for your students. They are brilliant.

"Your daughter is brilliant. Thing is, your daughter is uninspired."

"But what if I ruin her life if I don't send her to high school with her friends?"

"Fair enough, but if you're brave enough, you'll ask yourself the flip side of that question."

Many years have passed, but the mother's words resound-like our conversation happened a moment ago.

I was employed at the time by a private high school as a part-time art instructor. Midyear the director asked me to oversee the sixth period study hall. I took on the job and quickly realized why the previous teacher had quit. This was not a study hall. This was a free-for-all.

Something had to give. I quickly did my own homework, gathered all the information I could about each enrollee's individuality and made an effort to let each student know that I cared. In the process I established a measure of trust. And as they began to trust my authority, the classroom began to calm down.

What is tremendous is that, to this day I remember these young men and women not for their academic accomplishments, but for their dreams. I was privileged to read the poem tucked inside the math textbook, to see the sketch that had gone unnoticed, to listen to the big ideas brewing.

One afternoon, a mom wandered in before the bell to find her son. "Are you the teacher?"

"Yes," I stretched out my hand.

"Oh, I am so glad to meet you. I just want to thank you for encouraging my son. I know he's not super smart and may never amount to much, but he speaks highly of you. It is the first positive feedback about school I have heard from him in years."

"Thank you... but you're wrong. Your son is brilliant."

Another teenage girl comes to mind. She had been expelled from high school because of her rebellious behavior. This girl was a juvenile delinquent, the real thing, the kind that climbs out of her bedroom at night to rave, the kind that gets arrested for possession. Still, when I sat across the table from her, looked into her eyes there was a glint of self, begging to be released. So I agreed to work with the family under clearly delineated conditions. Tragically, the scene ended as quickly as it began.

While it was clear in that short span of time that this was an intelligent girl, she simply did not have the tools to respond to her intelligence. This teenager was caught in a conflict between the need for social-emotional acceptance and the interior whispers of a shriveling self. You can guess which need had the stronger drive.

Her parents were socially-emotionally driven too. Their overwhelmed schedule often left the adolescent to her own devices. It's not that her parents abandoned her; they simply trusted blindly that the school system would cultivate their daughter's individuality. Mom and Dad spent much of their time engaged in volunteer activities while their daughter spiraled in crisis.

Flannery O'Connor's short story, "The Lame Shall Enter First," comes to mind:

> The tripod had fallen and the telescope lay on the floor. A few feet over it, the child hung in the jungle of shadows, just below the beam from which he had launched his flight into space.[2]

I was jolted into the gravity of the situation at hand, stunned by these parents not being able to dismiss even a fraction of their activities to nurture their relationship with their daughter.

When is it too late?

I suggested that their daughter needed both her parents to actively participate in the process of re-directing her acting out. This teenage girl needed active parenting. I saw potential that, tragically, neither she nor her parents were willing to protect.

This girl was not the first. The larger sorrow, I fear, is that this story rings true for many a teenage girl.

pandemic

I'm sitting across the table from someone's 14-year-old daughter.
You know, the one who wants to be the lucky girl in the arms

of a naked Abercrombie model? She's the girl who wears a stolen
pair of jeans to look the part, the one waiting to be sentenced

for her crime. With a cell phone tucked between her breasts, poised
for her lover's call, she's drenched lackadaisical in never-ending

due dates, No. 2 pencil darkening bubbles that don't matter.
This girl has never learned to read. There is no time to paint

her very own Mona Lisa. The scene is slow motion, macabre:
I'm flashing my Morse code mayday, praying that reinforcements

will arrive in time, all the while wondering what on Earth
might soothe the grenade drooling in the palm of her hand.

Beware: Author and expert on creativity and innovation in education and business, Sir Ken Robinson, has been raising his voice for more than a dozen years to warn us that creativity has been exterminated from the classroom. His message is judicious:

> Our own times are being swept along on an avalanche of innovations in science, technology, and social thought. To keep pace with these changes, or to get ahead of them, we will need to have our wits about us—literally. We must learn to be creative.[3]

Formulaic methods are creeping like ivy across education boundaries to sap the life out of learning.

Public, private and home schools are at risk of promoting uninspired students, which will result in all sorts of havoc, but the more significant dilemma is the fact that our children are being sapped of their individuality.

My husband's parents shower me with trinkets from their travels — rich bits of the wide world.

After an adventure to Turkey they shared how every person they met invited them to stop for tea to enjoy a moment of kinship.

"Stop everything? Wouldn't that be nice? How?" I interrupted.

"Well... they are prepared."

I went straight home set on adopting a Turkish tea tradition. I set my grandma's teapot, the matching creamer and sugar bowl on a wooden tray in plain sight. I added to the mix a basket of loose leaf Assam, a tea strainer, and little silver spoons for stirring. I was ready to enjoy the company of the very next person who dared to cross my threshold. I'm not sure what happened to that tray in the flurry of life.

Another time, my in-laws brought me a book all the way from The Czech Republic. Truth of the matter is, I'm writing these artifacts from the guild because of that little book they tucked into their carry on.

I Never Saw Another Butterfly is a collection of poems and illustrations crafted by children during their internment at the Third Reich's propaganda ghetto: Theresienstadt. Over the course of three and a half short years 15,000 children were patted on the back and prodded through the ghetto's gates to the open arms of the Holocaust. Only 100 children survived. Their art will stand the test of time. Their art will simply not allow their cries to diminish. The volume is up, this testament is loud and clear, "Only the shot-down birds tell of war".[4]

How did this happen?

Student of the Bauhaus, mentored by the likes of Johannes Itten and Paul Klee, Friedl Dicker-Brandeis designed textiles, furniture, elaborate costumes, and theatrical sets. But above all else she was a teacher. She taught children drowning in hopelessness to utilize the language of art to ease their burden. She taught them to leave the world a gift: a flicker of their soul fluttering on butterfly wings.

When, on December 14, 1942, Friedl Dicker-Brandeis was deported to Theresienstadt, she chose to spend the last two years of her life inside that ghetto teaching hundreds of children to reach into their hopelessness, translate it into poetry and visual art, and in so doing release their pain. She also taught them to raise their voices:

> The children waited for her quietly, eagerly. She did not know Czech and only spoke German, yet that didn't seem to matter. She taught the way she had been taught by her art teachers in Vienna and the Bauhaus: exercises in breathing and rhythm; the study of reproductions, texture color values; the importance of observation, patience; the freeing of oneself from the outer world of numbing routine and the inner world of dread.[5]

This teacher understood that the power of creativity is not extracurricular; for it unshackles the hopeless, exposes what lurks in darkness, and has the power to speak the unspeakable.

The students of Friedl-Dicker-Brandeis left us 2000 paintings and poems in a suitcase that testify to the profound potential for genius in every child. And we don't have time to cultivate individuality in our classrooms? Really?

Maybe we should read between the lines of the graffiti that scribbles our neighborhoods. Might this misdemeanor be the creative expression of an individual pleading for purpose?

In the fall of 1944, on October 6, Friedl Dicker-Brandeis was deported to Auschwitz via transport Eo No. 167. She died at Birkenau three days later, this woman who taught children to soothe the nightmare.

girl with raised fists

> "Today only one thing seems important — to rouse the desire towards creative work, to make it a habit, and to teach how to overcome difficulties that are insignificant in comparison with the goal to which you are striving."
>
> *–Friedl Dicker-Brandeis*

herded into a departing transport, the artist is
lugging Bauhaus in a suitcase

adding bruises to rubble, jackboots
scavenge a pocket watch and loose coins

as crayon and bristles, tempera and scraps of paper
hold their breath in her satchel

forced to journey barefoot on an icy road,

she paints them a lullaby in a cage of crackling
barbed wire,

    the children whose
    bones are
    drowning in
    striped pajamas

she urges them to reach for blue that swaddles
yellow stars in a shriveling sky

sets them sailing, on little red boats,

    their candles tatting light
    as the train whistle
    splits the night

The intent of education is to impart the tools that will allow the individual to explore their individuality, to discover pockets of the real world — math, charity, science, patronage, art, technology, history, music, compassion, and other marvels.

When did we decide that discovery is not necessary?

Why, instead of filling the mind with tools, do we fill the mind with everything already discovered?

Why, instead of producing explorers excited to make their way in the world have we produced a generation content to explore a virtual world in a sterile room?

Why do we insist that children memorize information to get a passing grade instead of walking alongside them to experience, own, or even reject the information they're being presented?

Our goal has changed: we have somehow substituted *how to think* with *what to think.* We are facing a serious problem in education today. Who will mentor the visionary individual? The noise is cacophonous. I hear Friedl Dicker-Brandeis whisper above the roar.

> Why do adults want to make children be like themselves as quickly as possible?... Childhood is not a preliminary, immature stage on the way to adulthood. By prescribing the path to children, we are leading them away from their own creative abilities and we lead ourselves away from understanding the nature of these abilities.[6]

The solution is simple, but the cost is high. We cultivate genius in every child when we inspire the heart, nourish the mind and train the will to actively engage learning with imagination. I don't presume this manifesto to be a "how to" or "rescue" manual. Rather, my hope is to begin a journey with anyone brave enough to walk the rugged path. This might seem an uncomplicated message but I find myself facing a morass of teaching methods that are indifferent to the individuals they purport to educate. When we fail to unlock the potential of a child's individuality we fail as educators.

> Friedl-Dicker-Brandeis understood the fragility and capacity of childhood. She wrote to a friend in 1940, "I remember thinking in school how I would grow up and would protect my students from unpleasant impressions, from uncertainty, from scrappy learning".[7]

O, to echo her wisdom.

TWO / *Begin at the Beginning*

Would you believe me if I told you that my philosophy of education began on the school bus?

During high school I bookmarked my days by slinking into a space that allowed me to exercise my contemplative nature. During that two hour commute, my senses were free to grapple with the real world, "What if I was the girl in that passenger seat? Who is looking out those skyscraper windows? Why is the man wrapped in rags perched on a crate, day in, day out?"

I don't remember much about completing the prescribed course of education; I do remember what I learned on the bus. There wasn't a chalkboard, there was no textbook to study and there was never a stitch of homework, but the bus was brutally academic.

My high school cohort traveled twenty seven thousand miles over the course of our three-year stint, spent about two thousand hours on that bus. I never was a brilliant math student but I'm pretty sure if you compress this to a single block of time it would amount to forty-five days of our lives.

Back in the 1980s, "Let the Good Times Roll" was blasting on KLOS, and KLOS was always blasting on the bus. I knew all the mile markers by heart. Exactly six stops past mine, bus doors swung open and Boy Stranger crossed the threshold from his world to ours. Sporting Mister Rogers' sweater, hair slicked back to the 1950s, lips whispering to no one in particular. Somehow I doubt there was ever a beautiful day in his neighborhood. Fighting his way through rapid-fire spit wads, crumpled paper bombs, and muffled sniggers, the teenage oddity desperately sought a seat in an environment intolerant of nerds.

His eyes were fixed on something none of us could see. Maybe that's what scared us. And if one of us was scared, all of us were scared.

Each morning, when he entered our scene, I wanted to escape to a world where nerdy boys are free. But more often than not, petrified by sneering peer pressure, I would set imagination aside, melt into vinyl and seize my guard, hoping the others would not see me watching him approach.

He was the embodiment of everything we did not want to become. As long as we didn't spiral to the level of Boy Stranger we would survive.

No one wanted to share their bus bench with Boy Stranger. Still, each day, breath held, limbs frozen, I secretly longed for his imagination to seep into mine. When, by default, I was the lucky body forced to slide over on the bench, I would roll my eyes for show, and budge, too weak to associate with Boy Stranger on an observable plane. But, in whispered tones, we delightedly chatted about school schedules, lunch box innards, and bits of imagination.

I confess. I was conflicted.

When we arrived at our destination deep within the city, tucked safely behind barbed wire, I stumbled to my first class and tuned out the teacher, attempting to tame a tangle growling wild, "Why is Boy Stranger not one of us?"

And here I am, thirty years later, compelled to pull at the beast of tangled threads with all my might.

Not long after high school I learned that Boy Stranger committed suicide.

Back then, being part of the crowd defined self. Loyal to the collective clique, I shunned Boy Stranger. Life is complex and I imagine there is way more to Boy Stranger's story than the thousands of erosive hours spent on the bus. But was the bus a tipping point? No one should have to endure twenty-one thousand miles of rapid-fire spit wads, crumpled paper bombs, and muffled sniggers.

So here I am, all grown up three decades later trying to unravel a tangle, "What could have made a difference?"

Maybe nothing.

Maybe me.

I often ask myself, "How did I get here?"

As a child I filled journals to overflowing, trying to make sense of the life that swirled around me. I didn't know it then, but I was forming a priceless habit. I didn't learn to write in school, the chaos of childhood taught me to write. Words were my lifeline. Each word, each phrase painstakingly crafted, was sparking catharsis. It was the process of becoming a writer that gave me the courage to press into the process of becoming an individual. The process of crafting words built prowess into my being enabling me to discover, bit by bit, my true self.

Each journey is unique and mine is no exception. While I loved the college experience and explored all sorts of subjects – from philosophy to biopsychology to ceramic sculpture – I avoided the realm of pedagogy. I wasn't exactly sure what I would become when I grew up, but I knew one thing for certain: I would NOT become a teacher.

Once upon a time, in a small town in central California I turned a corner and the next thing I knew, "*Poof!*" I was a teacher. The story goes something like this: My daughter Hannah was entering kindergarten, a friend of mine who taught in a small private school was seven months pregnant and needed a long term substitute. I got the job. Funny thing, I don't remember applying. It seems my unique education background and life experience trumped the teaching credential.

When, in the first grade, my daughter was not allowed to read books above the average level of the other students in her class, my new career got interesting. I tried to use logic with my colleagues, stating that Hannah's precocious reading ability would certainly raise the bar, spark some healthy competition in the classroom. Their reasoning was that Hannah posed a threat to her classmates' self-esteem. Meanwhile, my daughter was waking up with stomachaches. I had to come to grips with the fact that Hannah was a disillusioned first-grader. My teaching career took a sharp turn at this unexpected bend in the road.

Looking back, Hannah's teacher had simply not been trained to recognize, let alone inspire, the creative impulse in my daughter. Her teacher could not imagine that she was tamping down Hannah's imagination by not allowing her student to explore an activity that she was independently motivated to explore. Cultivating student independence is not a central priority in the classroom; yet, the consequence of leaving the individual's creative process to stifle is, I imagine, leading to nervous stomachs in countless classrooms.

When I turned that corner and became a teacher, I enrolled in my own private university at the kitchen table. I researched elementary pedagogy by the light of the moon. I began with the catchy titles: John Gatto's *Dumbing Us Down* and Gardener's *The Unschooled Mind: How Children Think And How Schools Should Teach*. I moved on to Maria Montessori, John Locke, Plato, and Piaget. I was mesmerized by their thoughts. I spent hours evaluating the state standards of not only California, but the standards from a host of states. And no, I was not satisfied knowing what was listed in those standards, I wanted to understand the *why* behind the seeming no rhyme, no reason lists of targeted objectives. I struggled to comprehend how a daunting numerical outline of task-oriented goals—thirteen years worth—could possibly blossom individuality. So I went to work evaluating how well meaning public and private educators animated these goals in the classroom. I was basically earning myself a PhD in Ed Philosophy without the validation of a diploma, scraping together tuition of blood, sweat, and tears.

Exploring the potential of creativity in education to promote individuality has enabled me on a personal level to slay demons that discouraged me from developing my own individuality as a young person. From an early age I understood that school needed reforming. The process of becoming educated simply did not teach me how to interpret and develop all the ideas that flooded my mind. Tragically, by the time I entered high school I was a pale version of my self. I suspected that my imagination mattered, but I had little confidence. School had taken my wherewithal.

I did not stand on my own two feet again to strengthen the muscles of my own creative intelligence until I began fighting to inspire the creative intelligence of my students. As I press into the work of responding to my own imagination, I am encouraged to challenge my students to do the same. Each day for more than a dozen years I've labored to inspire the hearts and nourish the minds of my students, only to discover my own heart inspired, my own mind nourished.

I am thankful for a long ago lucid moment one night on a plane somewhere between New York and Los Angeles when I experienced the peace of accepting my true self without the entanglement of self-conscious insecurity for the very first time. The year was 2003. I turned 40 that year. I had spent the better part of ten years imagining and operating a prototype cooperative classroom before launching a fully equipped school in Los Angeles. By year two, our student population doubled. But tragically, I realized I was entangled with a Board of Directors who were not willing to continue the challenging work of promoting an academic program dedicated to developing critical creative thinking in students.

I was devastated by an increasing divide and wanted desperately to make this board recognize the significance of the progress we were making in the classroom guild. But I would not succumb to the pressure to conform to a standardized approach.

Drawing from the well of what I'd learned to be true about the pursuit of creative endeavor gave me the courage to press on. Admittedly, when the walls began to crumble, I hid in the janitor's closet for a few weeks during student drop off and pick up to avoid confrontation, but I eventually mustered some courage and crawled out of my fear.

When I did, I took a deep breath, stood firmly on two feet and booked a plane ticket to NYC to fellowship with like-minded, albeit dead, painters.

I traveled across the country to spend a few hours eavesdropping on a visual conversation between Henri Matisse and Pablo Picasso.

As they spoke to one another, long ago, in a call and response of oil on canvas, I'm sure they had no idea that their intimate exchange would one day be joined by countless others. I may have begun my relationship with them as an eavesdropper, but, as I watched them bare their soul to one another, I felt as if I had been welcomed and asked to participate.

I'm pretty sure I heard them whisper a double dare, "We must talk to each other as often as we can".[8]

A seed was planted, an idea born.

I collected a trinket, a small plate adorned with Picasso's *Peace Dove* at the Guggenheim to help me remember my journey's purpose before charging off to the airport.

On the plane, somewhere over NYC bound for Los Angeles, I experienced that peace. I did something I hadn't done in years: I wrote a poem.

I would land empowered at LAX, Madeleine L'Engle whispering in my ear, "From Aristotle I learned that a story must have a beginning, a middle and end. That, as the Red King advised Alice, it should begin at the beginning, go on to the end, and then stop. That when we are at play, or looking at a painting or a statue, or reading a story, the imaginary work must have such an effect on us that it enlarges our own sense of reality".[9]

Looking back, the purpose of the trip ended up being much greater than I imagined at the time. While the Board of Directors might have the power to knock down the walls of our school, my weekend of being mentored by Matisse and Picasso taught me that true teachers reach beyond walls. Matisse and Picasso patted me on the back and reminded me that I, too, am a mentor.

I marched into the war zone of a school falling apart at the seams and spoke from the heart, using pitchers of water and a tray of assorted glass jars to demonstrate my belief that education is the act of pouring possibility into an eager vessel. Sadly, the metaphor was lost on the group of angry administrators.

Though I grieved the lost potential, I accepted an offer to continue the work of empowering children to cultivate their individuality safely inside my living room.

Home again, daring to explore the classroom guild.

A large part of the battle we face in education today is required adherence to a schedule that prevents students from exploring their creative impulse. Education does a disservice to culture at large when it regards creative pursuit as extracurricular.

We aren't trained as educators to utilize imagination in the classroom. Stepping outside the box is not exactly the answer. I'm pretty sure we need to dismantle the box. The problem with traditional models of education is that they fail to recognize not only the relationship of imagination and higher thinking, but more importantly they fail to recognize the student's capacity to imagine. Creativity is a form of intelligence as worthy of pursuit as any required core subject and is, in fact, necessary for students to thrive.

Math never captured my imagination as a child until I had a teacher who spoke of the subject in real terms, a man who introduced me to Fibonacci and Archimedes. What happens when children are allowed to experience music, experience literature, experience visual art, allowed to experience math?

Well-meaning educators are tamping down the ability to engage critical creative intelligence. When students are not taught to value and respond to the creative impulse that prods them to wonder about the world, creators of original thought in the field of math, poetry, philosophy, science, and the arts are lost. Luckily I had the tenacity to chase the creative impulse without the encouragement I craved. "No Child Left Behind" implies that no child will be left behind in math, no child will be left behind in reading, no child will be left behind in science. What if the focus becomes discovering that unique something intrinsic to each and every child's nature and not leaving that unique something behind? Attending to the protection and promotion of the creative impulse in the child is the way to achieve this goal.

The best gift my grandmother ever gave me was a dinky portable typewriter. I remember opening the gift, delighting in my good fortune, and getting to work straight away making mailboxes out of cardstock and tape to hang on the interior doors of my grandparents' home. A newspaper was born.

The feel of the keys, the plunk, plunk, plunk, comforted as I whiled away childhood night after night. Being born into a frenetic family, life was often tumultuous. *The Friday Night Flash* was a delightful diversion. The little paper proudly endured a decent run of three years and shut down in the black, having earned $5.75 in profit (which is more than can be said for some monolithic publications).

I was struck with a cosmic revelation when my grandmother died and I stumbled upon a box that contained a sizeable archive. She had saved a copy of each and every edition of my paper. Silently stunned, staring down at the aged collection, a wispy image of her, gleefully chuckling, paper in hand, came to mind. My words mattered.

I often wonder what gave me the tenacity to publish that little paper. I grew up in a home with a television in every room. I believe the creative impulse exists in all children. Even a house full of blaring TV's couldn't stop me from responding to my own imagination. But I shiver to think of the children whose creative impulse shrivels because they are not encouraged to listen and attend to the whisper. What is to become of children whose ideas are drowned out by electronic distractions?

While my grandmother's affirmation was not directly intentional, discovering her archive of my little newspaper was tremendously affirming. I strive to affirm my students pro actively as they press into the work of developing their individuality. As a child I was curiously aware of my creativity. I suspect most artists are.

Childhood is precious.

As educators we must be mindful of what happens when we don't affirm the individual.

Because three of my four children are musicians, I listen to a wide array of music. I am fascinated by what songwriters are communicating. My daughter is not only a classically trained pianist and a composer who aspires to write for film, but her musical listening skills are broad and acute.

She thinks deeply about music. Hannah is not only a music major, but a history major in a Socratic Honors program at her university. She recognizes that music, historically speaking, has its finger on the pulse of culture at large. So when Hannah suggests I listen, I listen.

Several years ago she introduced me to Arcade Fire, "Mom, you really should listen to 'Wake Up'."

My reading of the lyric made me want to shout to the world, "Listen to this...!"

While this, most certainly, is not a song about education, the sentiment is eerily parallel. What happens to the child's individuality when they're taught that learning is comprised of collecting facts? At some point they will wake up to the fact that their individuality has suffered.

A student succumbing to dissuasion is an ever-present danger in the classroom. As an educator, I gather much from my reading about the creative process that is applicable to students in all subject areas. From *Art and Fear*, by David Bayles and Ted Orland, I discover that an underlying principle of the creative process is risk:

> After all, wanting to be understood is a basic need—an affirmation of the humanity you share with everyone around you. The risk is fearsome: in making your real work you hand the audience the power to deny the understanding you seek; you hand them the power to say, 'you're not like us, you're weird; you're crazy.[10]

Providing opportunities for students to risk, develops the prowess that will enable them to discover, bit-by-bit, true self. The process of exploring imagination is a worthwhile journey because the process of discovery is glorious.

If we are being honest, the truth of the matter is, one day we all must come face-to-face with who we are at the depth of our being and consciously decide to either promote that self or leave it by the wayside.

I realized early on that the process of earning my MFA as a forty-something student was not so much about the degree as it was about embracing my individuality.

why i am

after Frank O'Hara

If I'm not a poet, if I'm not a painter,
why am I? I think I would rather be
a poet, a painter, but I'm not. Oh well.

For instance, in the kitchen
I imagine a painting when something
slips between the bars, "Sit down,
have a slice of pie," I say.

I eat; we eat. I look up. He says, "You don't have
BRICKS in it."

"Yes, I crave something there."

"Yes, *you do*."

I go on and the days go by
and he drops by for pie again and again
and again. The painting
is going on, and I go on and on, and the days
go on and on and on so I knead some yeast
and flour and water. I lyric a dough.

I rub the excess from my hands
onto my fading calico apron

because the painting is not BRICKS
at all just a rotting orange carved
with a mass of font.

"You're not a poet,"
"You're not a painter,"
he reminds me, pie drooling
from the corners of his mouth.

So one day I'm thinking of BRICKS
and rotting oranges. I take an ax to canvas,
a brick-orange ax. Pretty soon orange peel
stained stanzas litter the kitchen linoleum—
marmalade, no rhyme. But there should be
so much more, not of BRICKS
not of oranges, not exactly words,
not exactly paint. I remember
the ax dripping brick-orange
tears, remember the pie eating demon,

how terrible are kitchens
and life. Days go by and on
and on until I see it is a canvas and
a canvas of poems rattling in my head:
still life with rotting orange and a BRICK.

And one day in a gallery I stare down the drooling
pie-eater,

"I am a poet and a painter."

I am haunted by a needle popping on a scratched copy of "Tea for the Tillerman," watching rain drip down the side of a classroom that was made of glass. I remember my 4th grade teacher's voice bellowing doom announcing that the art and music teacher would not be visiting anymore because funding (whatever that meant) had been cut. I remember my interior voice screaming, *"What will happen to people like me?"* Beyond feeling personally rejected by the pronouncement, I have a vivid memory of becoming indignant for the multitude of children who would not be taught to value creativity, who would not be taught to respond to the creative impulse. *Injustice!* Images from long ago continue to inform my steps.

My grandmother who raised me was a trained dancer and a talented illustrator. She made her living as an executive secretary. "Creativity is great for playtime," she said, "but it is not serious work." My grandmother was wrong. It was serious to me. My ideas were so strong that I couldn't ignore them. Creativity was not a whisper but a roar. Tragically, I was never given the tools to respond. As a mentor, I am forced to respond to my own creativity to teach my students to understand that their ideas are worth attention.

Driving in downtown Los Angeles, I recognized the mascot of the forest service. Smokey Bear had settled down at a bus stop. He nodded as I passed. Guess he turns 65 this year.

Back in the '70s, when I was in elementary school, three generations of women in my family—my mom, grandma, and great-grandma—did something unprecedented, something that would never be done again to the best of my recollection. They crafted. Back then, decoupage was all the rage. The matriarchs of my family took this art form to a whole new level, rescuing abandoned planks of wood and charring them on the open flames of our harvest gold gas stove. They invited me to join them for hours upon end at the kitchen table as they cut images from food and family magazines and arranged them with artistic flair on the bits of blackened wood. All three women exhibited their work in their respective kitchens.

When Smokey Bear visited my classroom to announce an art contest, almost immediately, I vividly envisioned my entry. I jumped off the school bus at the end of that day and ran to my grandma's arms, "Can we make a Smokey plank?"

I remember working together in the kitchen. We were four generations of creative women at work on a political poster. I remember being encouraged by my mom, my grandma, and my great-grandma as I drew an enormous Smokey first with pencil, then with markers until he was just right. When it came time to burn the plank, they taught me how to be safe with fire. Smokey would have been proud.

The day I took Smokey to school, all three women waited for the hydraulic sigh of bus doors, patted me on the back, and smiled, "Good work." But the story does not have a happy ending. When I turned the project in to my teacher, she looked stunned then scolded, "You did not create this on your own."

My teacher simply could not imagine that a child could so cleverly juxtapose a burnt plank with Smokey Bear. I wanted to scream, "This is my work!" I didn't care if I won a prize. I had basked in the rare experience of my family mentoring my creativity and this teacher's negative comment wanted me to feel ashamed. My teacher failed to recognize that some things are more important than a contest.

Today, Smokey Bear, on a remote corner in downtown L.A., caught my eye to remind me that I spend my days encouraging students and their teachers to explore their imagination because of that teacher who long ago undervalued my imagination. So here I am, the teacher who spends her days echoing Smokey's cry, "Only you can prevent wildfires." Guess I won a prize after all.

While founding academics on creativity is, at times, a challenging (not to mention loud) approach to education, it affords our students ample opportunity to develop critical creative thinking abilities. Often I pause in my tiny classroom to soak in the glorious buzz. The very nature of our school is unique—a place where children of many ages independently explore their world by interacting with the arts, sciences, and humanities.

We recognize that the complexities of measurement can be taught by observing gauges on a car's dashboard, so we drive a literal mile to measure the real world. Using a spool of string to compare the size of a blue whale to a dolphin or to decide whether the Mayflower will fit in the play yard, students live learning. Stretching a 100-foot piece of string across the yard has an impact that will never be achieved by a two inch drawing in a book. We begin in the concrete to introduce complex, abstract concepts.

During the course of any day, I catch my breath because I have learned something fabulously imaginative from a student. Teaching is a mysterious symbiotic relationship: I gain creative insight from my students, dig into the work of creating based on what I learn, and in turn, bring the material back into the classroom in a form that they can explore. One rainy morning a few years back, I was commiserating with a teacher, exhausted in that moment by the never-ending administrative tasks of teaching. I was interrupted by a ten-year-old boy, *"Mrs. Bredberg! Mrs. Bredberg! Look! Look at the rain!"*

Both my colleague and I took two steps through the threshold to look up, causing our mundane routine to be sprinkled by droplets of spontaneous beauty. This is the boy who, at a patronizing glance, might be tossed off as a student who won't amount to much. This is the boy who skips into the classroom, slips into imagination like Lewis Carroll, and comes back with fistfuls of hope. In my opinion, this boy is brilliant. Sure he struggles with a narrow range of academics and social skills, but he works diligently at his weaknesses and progresses according to an individual timetable like all of my students. When we value imagination, we value the individual. Here is a boy endowed with a vivid imagination who is able to seamlessly and unself-consciously tap into its storehouse. Since that day, I have never taken the poetic potential of a rainy day for granted again. The moral of the story reminds me of Patricia Polacco's allegorical tale of Appelemando, the dreamer who brings color to a drab village, whose imagination is, "magic chariots pulled through his mind by galloping hues of color."[11] Imagination is always within arm's reach.

How far have we really progressed since Sir William Curtis made his toast to the 3Rs back in 1825? In a culture that purports to value diversity, how do we justify a primary and secondary education system that addresses only a narrow scope of skills—reading, writing, and arithmetic? In fact, standardized testing has sent creativity-in-the-classroom packing:

> "Teachers in pre-K—3rd grade increasingly focus on a narrow range of literacy and math skills, with studies showing some kindergartners spend up to six times as much time on those topics and on testing and test prep as they do in free play or 'choice time'.[12]

While we all agree that language and math literacy are vital to a thriving culture, I am convinced that training the student to discern and attend to the creative impulse is equally vital. What happens when the student is not provided opportunity to exercise critical creative thinking? Will the skill atrophy? What will be lost?

Many parents who cross my path are singularly concerned that their son or daughter be an exceptional student of math. While I'm a firm believer that every student who has ever crossed my path possesses *specific* genius, not every student who crosses my path possesses *math* genius:

With a bit of excavation, I often discover that these parents have experienced early childhood math anxiety and confess that the anxiety continues to haunt them. I have spent many hours conferencing with conflicted parents panicking about their child's math status: "Of course Amanda is a poet and, as her mother, I want her to press into the work of the poet... but what about *calculus*?"

I've referred many a parent like Amanda's to Frederick, Leo Lionni's fable about individuality and community. When the industrious mice realized their winter storehouse was barren, they turned to Frederick for sustenance, "Then they remembered what Frederick had said about sun rays and colors and words".[13] The poet dreamer saved the day.

Cozy...?

Every year in the spring, I hand my students two freshly sharpened Ticonderoga #2 pencils and begin the day by reading scripted instructions. Yep, standardized testing.

After years of administering these tests and receiving in return reams of graphs and charts communicating grade equivalencies and national percentile ranks for my students—numbers and pictographs that did not communicate the type of specific information that would help me instruct individual students—I decided to score the tests the old- fashioned way. I took the entire battery of tests myself, made a key, and corrected my student's tests to see what types of mistakes they made. Now I realize this is an unconventional tactic, one that might be frowned upon, but what I learned confirmed my teacher's intuition; it's impossible to measure creative intelligence on a standardized test.

Because my students are taught to approach all subjects critically and because the individuality of the test taker is not factored into the scoring of standardized tests, I stumbled upon significant ambiguity.

A case in point is Cloë's response after reading a passage about the Library of Congress. Cloë was a budding poet from the time she could hold a pencil and has grown into a teenager who crafts lines like, "I am brocade wallpaper/ Sliding off a plaster façade/Peeling away in square dreamscapes/Like the wallflower/I watch, I set traps/And the ivy is envious." She was the barefoot third grader who hauntingly recited Emily Dickinson to a mesmerized classroom of boys and went on to receive national recognition for her own poetry five years later. Cloë was a contemplative elementary student who was most content inside a great story. So when I read her response to the following question I burst out in warm laughter:

According to the passage, how would you best describe the Library of Congress?

a. cold
b. austere
c. cozy
d. dark

To Cloë, the description of the 200-year-old federal cultural institution, an enormous library, housing shelf upon shelf of rare books, resonated with pages straight from her imagination. I know this because I had been working with her to revise her creative writing:

> *Perched on a sturdy willow branch I watched fireflies dance in between gowns. I found myself completely bored until an hour before midnight when I wove my way into Lady Cordial's library. There I sat silently clutching my plate of half eaten trifle, reading the many nonsensical books she had collected over the years of training to be a versifier. Hours quickly passed until the library bell loudly reminded me that it was one o'clock. I tiptoed downstairs and was met by the ridiculing eyes of Maliesa. Not wanting to talk about how amazing she was and how horrible I looked in my potato sack of a dress, I escaped by accidentally dropping my dessert plate and running to fetch a broom.*
>
> *—excerpt from Cloë's, "Pins and Needles"*

There was absolutely no doubt in Cloë's mind that the passage about the Library of Congress described a place providing a feeling of comfort and warmth, that the question was best answered, "c" a "cozy" place. There is no doubt in my mind that according to the writers of the test, "b" an "austere" place was the desired response.

Cloë's answer was an intelligent, appropriate subjective response. The question on the test was ambiguous for this specific student. This was not an isolated case. As I dug into the test that spring, I found questions throughout the test that were ambiguous for specific students.

I've never gone to the trouble of scouring the test again. I learned what I set out to learn. I still dutifully administer the test each spring for exposure. But before I start reading the script, I tell my students the story of the "cozy" Library of Congress.

We need to prepare our students for every academic requirement they may encounter, while simultaneously preparing them to blossom into their uniqueness. Because advanced math, algebra, trigonometry, and calculus have become the standard, uniqueness has become compromised. This is a dilemma for the educator and a tragedy for the individual. Students not adept at math expend a significant amount of energy to take a test and receive the grade only to forget all they learned in one great sigh as they walk out the door. Could that energy be better spent?

I have a friend whose parents were educators. While I'm sure they loved their daughter, they simply would not tolerate her creative nature unless she performed at an above average level in math. My friend is not wired to be a mathematician. Consequently, after years and years of failing at math, she spiraled into a self-esteem crisis.

Recently, well into her fifties, after embracing her creative nature, she earned a two-year degree in painting from a community college and was accepted to UCLA where she was to complete her four-year degree, with one catch of course. Her acceptance was contingent upon completing statistics. Statistics for a visual art degree? *Really*?

My friend made it through college algebra after taking it twice and spending hours upon end with a tutor. She ran this gauntlet because she wanted to study painting. Sadly, she couldn't muster the courage to press into statistics. Math took the wind from her sails and she gave up on her dream.

There is an obsession about math in our culture. But the problem is larger than this small obsession. Our system of education forces students through a prescribed and severely limited course of study that has become a terrible diversion that crushes individuality.

We observe the essence of critical creative thinking in creators who are pioneering in their fields—scientists and painters, pianists, mathematicians, and the like. Helping students learn to not only observe the creative process but to put their observations into practice will allow them to transmit these skills to other fields of study. Whether it is from the need to feel and to make others feel, to innovate, to solve, whatever the unique motivation, creators press into their imagination. In so doing, they dare us to do the same.

Being mesmerized with the life and work of Van Gogh, I've had the privilege on more than one occasion to wander through mega exhibitions of his work—"Van Gogh's Van Gogh's: Masterpieces from the Van Gogh Museum" at LACMA and "Van Gogh to Mondrian: Modern Art from the Kröller-Müller Museum" at the Seattle Art Museum. I visit paintings in local museums regularly, "Irises" at The Getty, "The Postman Joseph Roulin" at LACMA, "Portrait of the Artist's Mother" at The Norton Simon, and "Hospital at Saint-Remy" at the Hammer. Though I mostly get lost in a private reverie pondering each canvas, I purposefully take time to step center gallery and watch how other people engage with the painter storyteller. Regardless of location—Seattle, NYC, Paris, Los Angeles—the scene is identical: People waiting in queue to grab crumbs from Van Gogh's table. Van Gogh believed, "Poetry surrounds us everywhere, but putting it on paper is, alas, not so easy as looking at it".[14] Whether he intended it or not, his exaggerated line, color, and texture demands we contemplate the poetry whispering in our midst—mistral vibrating trees and people with green faces. Reminiscent of Dorothea Lange's haunting images of Great Depression breadlines, I am struck by the purely unconscious drive of the viewers mesmerized by Van Gogh's work. I am struck by people craving something that can only be satisfied through the imagination of the artist.

Knowing of my fascination with the work of Flannery O'Connor, and my appreciation of Thomas Merton's contemplative musings, a friend recommended I read *The Life You Save May Be Your Own: An American Pilgrimage*. The title alone, alluding to a favorite O'Connor story, was enough to hook me. Reading Paul Elie's critical work, a frame-by-frame replay of a race that belonged to four mid-20th century American writers—Dorothy Day, Thomas Merton, Flannery O'Connor, and Walker Percy— I discovered men and women who were often uncomfortable in their own skin, who, nevertheless, pressed into and acted upon a nagging burden because they imagined a magnitude of possibility. These men and women were keenly aware of their creative impulse and could not help but pursue the burden to write in response to the world swirling around them.

I am a dedicated teacher, but I am also a dreamer like Dorothy Day, pressing into a long loneliness, an apprentice seeking the companionship of a master artisan. Reading this book was a turning point. As I eavesdropped on the creative journey of these dead men and women, they became mentors. My eavesdropping opened a door, sparked a connection: I was being invited to join a virtual guild. As I followed these creators on their journey and became privy to the creators that influenced their writing, I began to muse. What if I invited these men and women into my classroom? Witnessing these four authors respond to the creative impulse emboldens me to do the same, might my students, in turn, be similarly influenced? Paul Elie suggests that Day, Merton, O'Connor, and Percy were men and women on a pilgrimage.

> A great event has happened; the pilgrim hears the reports and goes in search of the evidence, aspiring to be an eye-

> witness. The pilgrim seeks not only to confirm the experience firsthand but to be changed by the experience.[15]

Honing their skills for the single purpose of passing a baton in the race set before them, the four began by looking back because "they saw themselves as representative figures"[16] compelled by the creative impulse and willing to do the work, believing it would contribute to a greater good. They sighted the batons of their forbearers– Dostoevsky, Tolstoy, Dickens, Blake, Kierkegaard, James, Melville, Hawthorne– and, motivated by a burden of influence, stretched their hands for a blind handoff, grabbed the thing, and ran, utilizing forward momentum to their advantage, recasting the universal elements of story into a shape that was relevant to a new audience, believing that story holds the potential to communicate life purpose and the power to save lives. Yes! I was on to something.

Passion is infectious if we allow it to seep into our being. These four writers, heralds of sort, courageously challenge their readers to embark on a pilgrimage of their own. I grab the baton and challenge my students to the same. We dwell in a culture that often values conformity over imaginative choice. Engaging in the authenticity modeled by these four writers gets me out of the blocks and into the race. And so I train my students to become active learners, "Dorothy Day, Thomas Merton, Flannery O'Connor, and Walker Percy are holding out the baton, "Clutch it and run!"

In the solitude of night, I'm the apprentice wrestling with the creative impulse, knowing full well that my day job begins when the cock crows. I can't help but imagine the joy of having my work justified by that elusive committee. Night after night I gnaw the artist's ration and press into the lonely work, realizing that some things in life are not for the faint of heart:

> The world displays perfect neutrality on whether we achieve any outward manifestation of our inner desires. But not art. Art is exquisitely responsive. Nowhere is feedback so absolute as in the making of art. The work we make, even if unnoticed and undesired by the world, vibrates in perfect harmony to everything we put in it. In the outside world there may be no reaction to what we do; in our artwork there is nothing but reaction".[17]

Creativity is not limited to visual art. Math is creative. Physics is creative, so is reading, and writing. The creative endeavor is intrinsically rewarding but recognizing this fact is not automatic. For this reason, much of my effort in the classroom is spent cheerleading, *"Your work is valued, don't give up!"* We mis-educate when we default to the teaching of facts. Imparting the skills necessary for the child to think critically and creatively is paramount. This is accomplished over time as we provide meaningful ways for students to connect with learning.

Developing camaraderie with creators who have gone before has not only taught me to personally engage with my impulse to create, but has also validated my impulse to teach my students to listen for and attend to their creative impulse. This habit of eavesdropping makes me part of something greater than myself, and that is precisely what I teach my students in the classroom guild. Eavesdropping gives me the impetus to transform scribbled pencil scratches cross-hatched on a crinkled piece of paper beneath my mouse to verse.

When I look at a painting, listen to a musical composition, read a fictional work or a poem or a play, I am searching for substance to connect to my own work.

Recently, a brief exchange between characters from the first produced play of Tennessee Williams, *Battle of Angels,* captivated my imagination:

> Sandra: That's the graveyard, honey. It's situated appropriately enough, on the highest point of land in Two River County, a beautiful windy bluff just west of Sunflower River.
>
> Val: Why do you go out there?
>
> Sandra: Because dead people give such good advice.
>
> Val: What advice do they give?
>
> Sandra: Just one word—*live*![18]

Sandra and Val remind me that I look back to believe, I look back to be reassured, I look back to live, *"Make me a beast half as brave!"*

Watching the moon wane, I explore the crevices of history to commune with artists firmly established in posterity. Night after night, as the clock strikes twelve, I'm an apprentice in the guild, growing curiouser and curiouser, doing the work of the artist, following the lead of Lewis Carroll, Picasso, Patti Smith and Sophie Matisse, Paul McCartney and Dustin Hoffman, and, the writers who invited me to the guild in the first place: Merton, O'Connor, Day, and Percy. Because of this, my students understand Elie's charge:

> "The situation is established with a few strong strokes. Life is grasped whole and seen objectively. The drama is taken out of the author's mind and into the world. The setting is fixed. The action is joined in progress"[26]

and this makes wandering the often-lonely path of the creator worthwhile.

THREE / *Slumbering Genius*

When the word "genius" slips off my tongue into the scene, my audience shrugs their shoulders and nods patronizingly.

I suppose people like Albert Einstein and Leonardo da Vinci come to mind. I know, who can compare? But I believe that every child possesses the potential for genius. I remind myself that I'm in good company with John Gatto:

> ...I've come to believe that genius is an exceedingly common human quality, probably natural to most of us. I didn't want to accept that notion—far from it: my own training in two elite universities taught me that intelligence and talent distributed themselves economically over a bell curve... The trouble was that the unlikeliest kids kept demonstrating to me at random moments so many of the hallmarks of human excellence—insight, wisdom, justice, resourcefulness, courage, originality—that I became confused. They didn't do this often enough to make my teaching easy, but they did it often enough that I began to wonder, reluctantly, whether it was possible that being in school itself was what was dumbing them down.[19]

I wouldn't say my job is easy, but interestingly, my students do demonstrate the hallmarks of excellence often enough that my job is a joy. The apprentices in my classroom guild achieve a tremendous level of focus because they have developed habits of being that enable them to value the work of attending to their creative impulse, work that often results in an original idea. And this original idea is the intrinsic reward that drives the student back into the work.

It seems to me that a large part of the battle we face in education is required adherence to a schedule that prevents opportunities for risk. Academic checklists have become the tyranny of the urgent. Consequently, many educators approach creative pursuit as extracurricular. I believe the study of creativity is vital as it will offer insight into individual intelligence. Promoting critical creative thinking is as worthy of pursuit as any required core curriculum and is in fact, necessary for genius to thrive.

When I peek inside the Renaissance guilds with my mind's eye, I see the likes of Michelangelo, Botticelli, Brunelleschi, Donatello, and I think to myself, "Every child possesses the potential for genius!"

Aren't we all capable of something exceptional?

What if genius is dormant in every child?

What if individuality is genius?

Individuality is risky business.

I periodically ask my writing students a simple question, "Where is the end of your world today?"

When I remind them, and I remind them often, of the Latin phrase found on medieval maps, *hic sunt dracones* which loosely translates, *beyond here, there be dragons,* I am asking them to explore a metaphor at length. This directive is part of an exercise I call, "Ready, write..." The challenge is to craft 750 words or less using *hic sunt dracones* as a title.

It is fun to see how these little entries transform over time. But more importantly, the exercise makes me wonder if simply being willing to go to the edge of the world has something to do with stirring the slumbering genius? I am pretty sure these writers are risking, even if the risk is only roughly imagined on a sheet of lined paper.

Critical creative thinking involves a significant measure of risk. Bringing original ideas to shape is not easy. The task is a messy, imperfect process. Helping my students understand that the creative impulse is valuable by helping them to make meaningful connections with creators gone before encourages them to risk.

Individuality is not always easy to embrace.

I imagine spending summers with my family at Dalguise House in Pertshire with Beatrix Potter. I imagine chasing Peter Rabbit down a lush Scottish lane.

But hoe in hand, all the chopping at clay soil I can muster does not a Dalguise garden make. I don't know what color my thumb is but it certainly is *not* green.

So I imagine a compromise. I stop fretting about the lawn in my front yard that manufactures crabgrass and settle on crafting miniature gardens in containers where the soil is controlled, *pliable*. I have, in my suburban plot of land, fashioned a satisfying eye-full of Scotland in galvanized tubs.

I have created a backyard biome for my children to observe nature in the city. We have worms, and moths, and butterflies, and June bugs, hummingbirds, and squirrels. We even have a rabbit named Greybone that goes *lippity lippity* in circles around the containers.

Greybone the rabbit

Salvia is a favorite in my garden—easy to grow and that lush purple hue, well, the image etched on my retina says it all. It had to be related to sage... I just knew it. Turns out I was correct. Those velvety leaves were a dead giveaway. I love these unkempt ornamental shrubs and their aromatic flowers that bloom and sway in panicles.

Salvia in my garden

Liam's favorite four-letter word is still d-i-r-t, so he jumped at the offer when I asked, "Hey, how about working in the garden with me today?"

"Sure Mom!"

We walk up the hill pulling the squeaky rusting wagon to the neighborhood nursery to pick up some plants for a handful of containers that need refreshing. I suggest Liam choose some plants for the raised bed near the front door.

"*Really*!!!" (His response warrants three, if not more, exclamation points).

"Yes, of course you can!" He sets out on a furious journey and is back again sooner than I expect with an armful of *Vinca*.

Vinca in my garden, too

The flowers flash in my face and make my heart sink. It's true. I am actually shocked by my response to this mass of cutie pie flowers. I mean, I have to engage in some serious and immediate introspection, "Vinca doesn't *match* the rest of the garden, is that it? No, I don't think so...that's not exactly the rub." I shake my head, snap out of it, and pulled it together for my lovely son, "Great Liam." I feel much better when I see his proud smile beaming from ear to ear.

Back home, Liam takes to task without a prompt. He turns the soil, digs holes with his bare hands for the tiny plants, pats them into their new home, and sprinkles the bed with water, all the while smiling cheerfully. *Cheerfully...* yes, that's it!

Liam chose Vinca because these flowers are just like him: *Cheerful.* And cheerfulness is not exactly the first word that comes to mind when describing me. I can *be* cheerful, but I am, by nature the Salvia melancholy sage. I am not the image of Vinca though I've longed to be that image at times. I truly believe that my gut response was because, in that moment when Liam lifted the mass of Vinca to my eyes, the flowers caught me off-guard and sneered, "You are *not* like us." And in that moment I slipped into an ancient insecurity.

But I'm the teacher who values individuality, even my own. I am thankful for the Vinca challenge that kept me on my toes that day. Sipping a glass of iced tea on my front steps, I smile at Liam's bed of Vinca, thankful for his cheerful nature, and then, when ice is left to jingle in the glass, I wander to my Salvia nearby.

It's time to launch a brand new school year. I open iPhoto to flip through images hoping to be inspired by antics past. I click through until I spy little Taylor with two of his elementary school buddies, "How cute."

taylor, robert, hunter before...

A few more clicks of the mouse and I pause at an image of the same three characters in their teens. I crack up.

Taylor, Robert, Hunter After!

And the common thread here is...?

Why, *individuality,* of course.

When education focuses on narrow outcomes, individuality is squelched. When we focus on promoting critical and creative thinking, individuality thrives.

I am glad to begin the year with the photo of three teenage boys playing dress-up.

Here's to more Mozarts, Batmans, and GEICO Cavemen!

We cultivate genius when we inspire the heart, nourish the mind, and train the will to actively pursue individuality.

Goals 2000 was beginning to be implemented when my oldest daughter Hannah was in Kindergarten. I received a cryptic postcard in the mail from the school district, a disclosure that the exit exam was on its way. In ten short years Hannah's graduating class would be affected.

These goals? All this by the Year 2000... *really*?

> *All* children in America will start school ready to learn
>
> The high school graduation rate will increase to at least 90 percent
>
> *All* students will leave grades 4, 8, and 12 having demonstrated competency over challenging subject matter including English, mathematics, science, foreign languages, civics and government, economics, the arts, history, and geography, and every school in America will ensure that all students learn to use their minds well, so they may be prepared for responsible citizenship, further learning, and productive employment in our nation's modern economy
>
> United States students will be first in the world in mathematics and science achievement.
>
> *Every* adult American will be literate and will possess the knowledge and skills necessary to compete in a global

> economy and exercise the rights and responsibilities of citizenship.
>
> *Every* school in the United States will be free of drugs, violence, and the unauthorized presence of firearms and alcohol and will offer a disciplined environment conducive to learning.
>
> The nation's teaching force will have access to programs for the continued improvement of their professional skills and the opportunity to acquire the knowledge and skills needed to instruct and prepare all American students for the next century.
>
> *Every* school will promote partnerships that will increase parental involvement and participation in promoting the social, emotional, and academic growth of children.[20]

I remember being fascinated by the specific goals the district had in mind, goals that seemed vague and far removed from my expectations of academics.

Being a concerned mom, I tucked the postcard into my purse and paid a visit to Hannah's Principal.

I began my show and tell. The Principal had never seen or heard about the information on the postcard. Flustered, he pulled an enormous binder from a stack on the shelf behind his desk. With a slam and a great puff of dust he proclaimed, "...must relate to this." The sad reality is that the discouraged Principal confessed, "Who has time to read?"

To rouse the slumbering genius, we must transcend such standards by inviting our students to ignite the potential of their individuality. Providing moments for students to experience the chaos of curiosity, teaches them that failure is the road to success.

I have three secret ambitions: To grow a garden that thrives, to learn to play guitar, and to become fluent in Italian. Sometimes my ambitions frustrate me, especially when I walk up the driveway, look to my left, and see the small plot of city dirt that holds the potential to feed my family as I rush to my computer to get cracking on another lesson plan. I become discouraged when I compare myself to Barbara Kingsolver, James Taylor, and Pavarotti (okay, so Italian is the stepping stone to opera).

I had a roommate in college who was a focused high achiever. While I had so many interests that I found myself spiraling into a state of indecisiveness, she had two activities on her free time list: exercise and cheesy romance novels. What I perceived as a lack of imagination kept her schedule even keeled. My roommate, who eased her way into a pediatric practice, was living the "can't do it all" kind of life that I secretly envied.

But the good news is I think I finally understand. As I press into the work of cultivating my individuality, I've made the conscious choice that there are some things that I simply cannot accomplish.

Our family enjoyed following the 21st Winter Olympics. I don't know what came over me last night, but when my

12-year-old son declared that he wanted to be a snowboarder like Shaun White, I blurted, "That is an unrealistic dream."

Did that really come out of my mouth? I am the creative educator who believes all things for her students! But the statement was at once freeing and bittersweet, like when you admit to your child that Santa is make-believe. In that moment I realized that I was empowering my son. I told him, "You can be a rock star, a songwriter. You can be a pilot, even an astronaut. But Liam, we live far from the mountains and don't have the resources to get to the snow every weekend. It is highly unlikely you will ever be an Olympic snowboarder."

I'm not a complete fun crusher. I went on to encourage my son that he shouldn't scratch snowboarding off his list of ambitions and dared him to reserve the dream of chasing gold for activities that are within arm's reach.

While watching the Olympics, I got the evil eye shot my way when Shaun White hit the bowl going for gold. I shot the mom glance back. Liam laughed. My son gets it. Liam is aware of what he can and cannot accomplish because he recognizes and values his individuality.

Gentlemen, start your engines!

Pinewood derby cars fall into two classes: those obviously made by kids and those obviously made by parents. A few years ago two of my sons built winning cars that fell into the kid made category but were viewed suspiciously because they won. Liam, too young to be officially eligible for a ribbon, built The Stealth, a car that beat every officially participating car.

Their dad showed them what to do but made them do the work. He passed his expertise to his sons and showed them how to implement everything from axle polishing to weight placement to wheel alignment. He gave them the knowledge and skill but required them to do the work with their own hands. This is a dad who mentored his sons and believed they could succeed.

In the end, the pinewood derby reminds me that I've observed three classes of teachers: those who don't bother because they do not think their students can succeed, those who do it themselves because they do not think their students can succeed, and those who truly mentor, passing on the knowledge and skill necessary because they believe their students can succeed.

Passing on knowledge is a noble purpose, believing in a child's potential, well, that is revolutionary.

My tale's no different than the next tale of personal combat—tangled in a twist, recuperating from battle at the end of the workday—except perhaps that I'm willing to chase a murmuring idea. When I look over my shoulder and no one's in the room, I imagine Mark Twain somewhere on the Mississippi charging me to throw off the bowline! I gladly take the wheel! Daring to engage in the work of becoming authentically me has enabled me to challenge my students to do the same:

Today six-year-old Mikayla, the youngest girl in school, watched me scale a countertop in high heels to fetch a pot for tea and observed, "My mom would never do that."

"I'm me," I replied.

This gave me an idea, "So what makes you, you?" Everyone in earshot eagerly chimed in (simultaneously of course):

I like to run, other people don't have to.

Different eyes and skin.

I like peanut butter, so does Michael, but Isaiah and Mikayla don't.

Dirt and lizards and pretty flowers.

I can eat what I like and you can eat what you like.

Writing a poem.

Computers and cars.

I can like math.

Ducks and monkeys and piano and drawing.

I like to read.

When I asked them to think about how school helps them become more fully themselves, the room was struck silent. Then, hesitantly, Mikayla whispers, "Courage."

"*Yes!*"

This little student, brave enough to raise her voice to a whisper joins Mark Twain's booming voice whispering through time.

Individuality is genius.

Though I teach many subjects each week, writing and visual art are by far my favorite because story is the core of all academic pursuit. Teaching students to become storytellers forces them to engage in a process that enables them to build habits that transfer to all academic pursuits. Learning is not about the grade, it's something connected to the soul.

My students understand this one classroom caveat: Individuality is a gift not to be squandered. Regardless of the academic domain we are tackling, they are confident that their imagination is relevant and so they work diligently to refine their voices by acquiring the habit of progressing methodically through the stages of the writing process. Though students may be annoyed by this type of practice, this type of practice is valuable.

I teach my students that it is not just practice that matters, but habits of being.

Children will readily share their dreams but what happens when we answer, "Yes you can," pat them on the back and watch them while away hours on the X-Box? Dreams shrivel when students form enduring trivial habits.

As the year wound down and I felt myself slipping into the usual panic wondering if we had accomplished enough, I took a deep breath and challenged my eyes to assess the situation. All around was evidence of accomplishment: a 275-page volume of original prose and poetry, a short film, a mountain of completed math lessons, history binders bulging at the seams, the remnants of a science fair, but it's the huge stack of dog-eared books, well-loved, that allows me to take in a sigh of relief.

Taking in the scene I was amazed. Each year I wonder how accomplishment of this magnitude is possible. "Routine," I whisper aloud. The accomplishment of each year happens over time, day by day, as the students engage in the framework of routine.

Fast forward, here I stand at the edge of August preparing lessons for a brand new school year. Why do I look back? I look back to remind myself that routine is not the enemy, routine is the hero.

Last week I had a conversation with a friend who teaches at a public high school in Los Angeles. As I was discussing the plans I have for my cooperative this coming year, specifically the literature we will explore, her bright countenance dimmed, "I only have the opportunity to read one novel per year with my students." We both stopped to acknowledge this very sad truth. This past year, my high school literature workshop explored eight novels. This coming year I have eight more slated to share with the group.

We are able to explore all those books because the routine for approaching literature is firmly established.

I see the snapshots in my mind.

I remember working with students to overcome the struggle to take notes, teaching the value of using vocabulary from the reading in a new context, reminding them to respond to comprehension questions with a complete sentence, and encouraging them to value their ideas about the story. I was helping them build habits, a routine that matters. Looking back, I see that applying these habits to each book allowed students to reach into their imagination and apply the great truths of the story to the real world.

Roots set deep into soil establish a framework for the tree to grow strong. When a routine rhythm of reading and exploring great stories is established from an early age, students will value the work of exploring books. And when this happens, individuals begin to engage with the deep reflection that leads to critical creative thought. Individuals must be taught to respond to their curiosity and to value the work of bringing shape to their imagination.

Rhythm and routine

The rhythm of routine provides the stamina to chase a dream, true, but individuality must be affirmed and cultivated. So as I ready myself to plan for a brand new year, here's a nod and a great "Hip, Hip Hurrah" to the hero of the day: Routine.

Recently I eavesdropped on one side of a phone interview: my son chatting with a staff writer for the *LA Times*. The resulting spread reminds us that there is indeed a link between the serious study of music and learning at large, "for all its beauty, power, and capacity to move, researchers have concluded that music is little more than ear candy for the brain if it is consumed only passively"[21] and goes on to suggest that,

> Learning *to make* music changes the brain and boosts broad academic performance. Findings across the board suggest that, even for a kid who will not grow up to be a Wynton Marsalis or a Joshua Bell, spending money and time on music lessons and practice is a solid investment in mental fitness.[22]

Of my son she remarks, "He is a kid with the attention span of an anesthesiologist, the persistence and discipline of an Olympic athlete, and the emotional range of an artist".[23] If she only knew the back story:

The right kind of practice...

What I see developing in my oldest son's character is something that a standardized test will never measure.

Taylor began tackling a concerto back in October. The process of moving from notes on a page to actual music was grueling, not only for him but for all the inhabitants of our home. For the piece to resemble music, he had to break the thing into sections to be played repeatedly. Whenever he made a mistake he would repeat that section... over and over, leaving notes to bounce off every square inch of wall and tangle somewhere in the center of my brain.

I was relieved when the notes were at last learned, thought I would enjoy 3 to 4 melodic hours a day. Nope. The next stage was to add dynamics, which entailed playing Ravel's ridiculously fast composition in fast motion... then slow motion through absolutely everything in between while stopping at sections where his fingers slipped to, you guessed it, fix each mistake three times. I pride myself a fairly patient person with broad musical appreciation, but any given section of this piece taken out of its entirety is fingernails on chalkboard. So this is how it went for three months straight.

When Taylor at last performed Ravel Concerto in G Major, III. Presto,

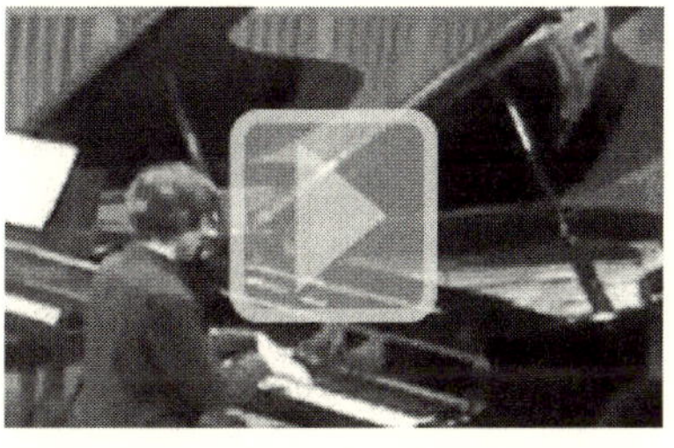

...makes perfect

(http://bit.ly/TB-Ravel)

I was shocked, "What?!!!" I had no idea! Then his music teacher's comment hit me on the head: "Taylor's come into his own."

"Come into his own? Who was it up to before tonight?"

It slowly dawned on me that the work of the teacher is implied in that overused phrase. As parents, Willie and I have never pushed or prodded Taylor to become a musician, but we have tirelessly encouraged him that his work matters. Taylor has worked hard to form this habit, but his teacher is right, he has at last embraced the work as his own.

My son Taylor is a normal 9th grade boy who did not read fluidly until the fifth grade, at which point he picked up *Harry Potter* and didn't stop until he completed the series. He is the boy who took spelling tests under the table and did his best to find the shortest way to craft a sentence because writing was so painful. He was the first grader who, left to his own devices, would spend hours standing on a stool experimenting with running water.

Last year Taylor, along with seven of my students, received recognition in visual arts *and* creative writing from the Scholastic Alliance for the Arts. Taylor won a state competition for an original musical composition for trumpet and piano entitled, *Something in Blue,* and recognition for an original film score. As a freshman in high school, Taylor is reading Tolstoy, learning Russian, and breezing through Algebra 2 by choice. Taylor is self-motivated.

Not only does Taylor play music, he *writes* music. This past week Taylor was sick and his one complaint was that he would not be able to work at his music... it's true.

We are ridiculously busy in this world, at times too exhausted to chase our own dreams. As a teacher, my students readily share their dreams of being a prima ballerina or an astronaut or a paleontologist, or, in the case of my son, a performing composer.

Creating Juilliard material was never our goal. Fighting for a habit of purpose is costly in more ways than one, but we find a way. There is no doubt Taylor's skill serves him well and hopefully will encourage others to engage in the work of animating a dream.

Confucius reminds me, "Learning without thought is labor lost, thought without learning is perilous".[24] As an educator, I believe promoting learning without creative thought and thought without creative learning leads to uninspired human beings. The creative process, far from being anti-intellectual is, quite the contrary, at its core the embodiment of critical creative thinking.

Those unfamiliar with the creative process assume that the act of creating is merely electricity emanating from the soul and disconnected from the mind. What the creator often agonizes over is not what comes from the soul, but how to translate what is in his soul in a way that is congruous with what he knows to be true in his mind.

The act of using what your mind knows to express what your soul feels is the essence of critical creative thinking. Teaching the creative process is not arts and crafts; it's not even a compartmentalized skill that can be outlined in a scripted scope and sequence. The creative process is a grossly overlooked core competency, a skill that, developed over time, will enhance any academic endeavor.

I am consoled by Madeleine L'Engle who reminds me that shaping a creative idea is not only a complex process, but a courageous act:

> I am grateful that I started writing at a very early age, before I realized what a daring thing it is to do, to set words on paper, to attempt to tell a story, create characters.[25]

Throughout my career as a teacher, I've never met a student who did not possess the mechanism to listen for the creative impulse and the desire to respond to that impulse. However, when students are not given the means or encouragement to respond, the student who once possessed the potential of becoming a creator runs the risk of becoming little more than a stunted regurgitator. Once, in a short story, I encountered a substitute teacher, Miss Ferenczi. I was mesmerized. Here was a teacher who led her students on expeditions into the imagination, "In higher math, which you children do not yet understand, six times eleven can be considered to be sixty-eight".[26] I wanted to ring up Miss Ferenczi and offer her a job. After reading Charles Baxter's "Gryphon" I imagine Frederick Buechner nodding in agreement:

> No matter how forgotten and neglected, there is a child in all of us who is not just willing to believe in the possibility that maybe fairy tales are true after all but who is in some degree in touch with that truth. You pull the shade on the snow falling, white on white, and the child comes to life for a moment.[27]

Attending to the creative impulse begins with ordinary facts, like six times eleven, but from there, as Miss Ferenczi courageously reminds us, it is the imagination that renders the possibilities limitless. Only when facts are filtered through the imagination are we able to recognize the extraordinary. Within the confines of a learning environment where the work of the imagination is affirmed, even the youngest students will confidently reach for the extraordinary.

Pysanky eggs

I remember Evelyn on the first day of kindergarten walking through my front door followed by her dad, video camera in hand. I remember her mom shooting me the glance, "It's time!" This year, Evelyn is a high school graduate. I closed the book on her transcript back in December. Recently Evelyn taught me how to connect the dots:

> Ever since my mom introduced me to pysanky egg making many years ago, I have been hooked. When Easter rolls around I have my friends over to create these brilliantly dyed eggs. Every year I get better and better and learn more helpful techniques. This year I was so ob-

> sessed with making eggs I would stay up 'till midnight painstakingly scratching on eggs with a wooden kiska.
>
> Ukrainian egg making teaches patience. It's a quiet, slow, endeavor but all the hard work and patience pays off. My favorite part of the process is when, after hours of work, I finally get to melt off the black wax with a candle and reveal the masterpiece!
>
> A few years ago we suffered a pysanky egg tragedy: Years worth of eggs had been left on the kitchen table while we were out to dinner one night. We returned to a floor covered in smashed eggshells. Our dog Jack had smelled the eggs and jumped onto a chair to get to the top of the table. He crushed them all.
>
> My mom cried. She's never gotten over the loss. I, on the other hand, just wanted to punt Jack down the staircase.
>
> Slowly we have begun to re-build our pysanky egg collection...

One spring I read all of Patricia Polacco's books to my students. After reading *Rechinka's Eggs* to our group, I heard my teaching partner, Sara, chime in, "We can do that."

The next thing I know we are blowing the insides out of eggs and teaching our primary aged children the art of batik. I find it interesting that the Ukrainian word "pysanky" comes from the verb "pysaty" which means to write. So picture teaching a group of 12 or so under ten-year-olds to write with wax on eggshells! Did I mention that there is fire involved in this activity? Yes, that's right, fire.

Here's the deal: children are capable. Was this activity chaotic? You bet. But not once did it cross my mind that this group of children was too young to engage in a sophisticated craft. Looking back, those young children proved that focus is not the issue. Children possess an incredible store of focus power, but we deny them opportunity to demonstrate their prowess when we don't believe in their ability to engage in complex tasks.

The art of pysanky teaches patience, true. When pure white shells—a tiny surface of potential—are painstakingly decorated, individuality emerges. All I can say is that this poet teacher sees a metaphor emerging.

My students are encouraged longitudinally to practice skills in an environment that echoes the guilds of the Renaissance. I am the mentor whose primary role is to help the apprentice form habits that matter. This is achieved by elevating process above content.

> The apprenticeship system, with its long period of study, early acquaintance with varied materials, copying, and collaborative work, somehow allowed boys who were probably quite ordinary in every respect to be turned into men possessing a high degree of artistic skill. Art—so the Renaissance believed—could be taught by a series of respective steps from grinding colors, to making copies, to work on the master's design, to inventing one's own paintings and sculptures.[28]

Teaching children to listen intently to ideas spinning in their minds and to develop storytelling skills enables them to engage in a miracle. I have a love/hate fascination with Emily Bronte's *Wuthering Heights,* have read the thing at least a dozen times and navigated scores of students through the mass of tangled heather and haze. Bronte's tale woven through a series of haunting flashbacks is a retelling of universal, albeit disturbing, truths about human relationship. What fascinates this educator is that growing up in the so-called stifling confines of Victorian England, Emily Bronte, her two sisters, and her brother somehow harnessed their imagination and engaged in the kind of practice that produced genius. As children, the Bronte's spent hours imitating and incorporating ideas of artists gone before them into their own imaginative creations.

To nurture genius in the individual we must provide a routine opportunity for children to explore imagination. Simply reading a book is a great place to start.

I read Beatrix Potter's, *Peter Rabbit* over and over and over with my firstborn, each time experiencing on a deeper level the simple yet profound message. Peter helped me gently impress on my daughter's heart the value of obeying people who love her. Mrs. Rabbit does not, after all, create rules so that Peter's life will be complete drudgery. Mrs. Rabbit lays down the law because she loves her little rabbit and does not want him to be in harm's way.

"More story, please!"

Once, while snuggling with three-year-old Hannah and reading a well-worn copy of the story, I was amazed when she grabbed the little book and began *reading* to me, "...but his sobs were heard by some friendly sparrows, who flew to him in great excitement, and implored him to exert himself." I guarantee she was not actually decoding, but I have no doubt she understood the meaning of all those big words. Three-year-old Hannah understood Peter's story on a deep level. We promote genius when we believe big things for our children.

We model the value of reading when we read aloud to our children. But is this why we read aloud to them? No! We read aloud to our children because story itself is wonderful.

Because I believe in the transforming power of story, when starting out as a Kindergarten teacher, my primary goal was to get children and their parents into the routine of reading. I've come to realize that reading with our children does not have to stop as they get older. We should never have to ask, "Remember the good old days when life was simple and we could snuggle up with our little ones to share the joys of reading a great story?"

When my daughter began reading chapter books on her own in the first grade, I did not want storytime to end, so, to her delight, I began reading the same books she was reading so that we could dialogue about the story. The characters and situations we encountered in these stories, afforded countless opportunities for me to mentor my daughter as she grew.

Reading *Peter Rabbit* over and over and over was the beginning of a habit of being.

Once their child is reading proficiently, people often approach me, "Do *I* have to read the book also?"

"No, you don't *have* to read the book, you *get* to read the book."

My next response is the memory of my pang of sorrow when Hannah began reading chapter books on her own.

When are children too old to share in storytime?

I was relieved when I realized that my response had to be a resounding, "Never!"

Reading and discussing great stories affords our family the opportunity to discuss situations that impact and affect the mind, heart, and soul.

With all this storytime remembering, it dawns on me that students have to believe in their ideas before they will engage in the work of putting them to paper. Books are the mentors that can show a student how to bridge the gap between a great idea and great writing. Everything read was first imagined.

In the landscape of language arts education, it is no wonder, with the loss of time to imagine, so many of my teacher friends are discouraged when it comes to teaching writing.

These professionals — quality, committed, exceptional teachers — are hitting the wall.

These well-meaning teachers are exhausted from teaching formulaic lessons that put their students to sleep.

Standardized lessons breed discouragement.

What if teachers had the freedom to move beyond predictable bell-curve outcomes and teach, not to the code, but to the individual?

Whether I'm addressing a classroom of public or private school teachers, or gathered in a living room with homeschool teachers, I begin by posing a question, "What if I told you I don't believe in writing instruction?"

Jaws drop, so I quickly segue so that the people in the room don't scurry out the door, "Seriously, how many of you encounter student resistance to the subject of writing?" At this point the vast majority of hands are raised. "Everyone is cursed when students hate to write."

"Instead of instructing students to approach writing as a formulaic problem to be solved, why not introduce them to the potential of their ideas."

When writing is taught by handing the student a collection of strategies — include 3 clauses, 5 active verbs, and a handful of qualifying adjectives here and there — the development of the writer's idea is drowned and the art of writing is reduced to selecting the appropriate combination of cookie cutters.

Writing must engage the reader, I remind them, "Teachers, we have somehow lost sight of our purpose: Great writing is a great gift!" I go on to explain that the student will learn from writing, a process that will transfer to any subject—math, art, history, science, literature, dance, and so on.

We need to teach three things no matter what is being taught. Fill in the blanks with any subject matter:

1. _____________ *is a tool to support your idea: Raise your voice!*
2. _____________ *is structured: Utilize the best structure to elevate your idea!*
3. _____________ *is a process: Keep moving!*

Just as no two fingerprints are alike, every author has a distinct writing style. Voice is the fingerprint of an author. But voice is also the mouthpiece of individuality and students who tap into their individuality are trailblazers.

A writer's workshop in the classroom guild begins with a simple question, "Why do we write?"

The standard response is, "To get a grade."

My response is always, "Writing is a gift you give to the reader."

Whether the work is scientific, analytical, editorial, fictional, or poetic, words should be crafted with an audience in mind. Communicating to my students to value their "voice" is a simple encouragement, but I have discovered it is key to unlocking all sorts of writer's block! When I say to my students, "Your writing has a tremendous one-of-a-kind voice," their faces beam. Helping students to discover this truth is foundational to the teaching of writing.

While effective writing may contain feelings and emotions, other times it informs in an encyclopedic fashion. Sophisticated writing often paints clever word pictures for the reader. Helping students keep an audience and purpose in mind helps them to become effective gift givers. Above all else, the reader should be able to sense sincerity, regardless of the purpose of the writing. Writing should be authentic and come straight from the heart. It is impossible to accomplish this goal with formulaic writing strategies.

Marks, symbols, and signs, word choice, the crafting of phrases, form, and rhythm all work together to bring a topic to life for the reader. This is a gargantuan task. When you get right down to it, writing is an abstract, complex, and somewhat mysterious craft.

Writers should become readers. Books are mentors. Digging into a great story, the young writer will discover all sorts of riches about the art of writing. Enabling our students to confidently develop and express their ideas, is a habit that happens over time. The habit begins when we connect young writers with great books and provide them with rich, relevant opportunities to practice writing an idea in response to their reading.

Through consistent opportunities to practice the art of writing, you challenge your students, "Let your beautiful voice ring!"

Parents are uniquely suited to recognize the individuality of their child.

When is it that we stopped believing in ourselves?

Often parents with children in academic crisis will call on me for advice. I begin with a challenge. I ask them to step back, to ask themselves who knows the heart of their child better, them or the expert?

Then I share a story.

When Hannah was three years old, I began to notice her left eye wandering. I immediately took her to our pediatrician who patted me on the back, "Oh it's nothing, she'll grow out of it."

But I knew it *was* something.

While Hannah absolutely loved for her dad or me to read her stories (she would actually sit for hours if only our vocal chords would allow) she did not choose to sit and flip through books independently as many of her toddler peers.

I decided to consult an *expert*.

I made an appointment with an ophthalmologist who took one quick look at her un-dilated eyes and told me that Hannah not only needed glasses, but she also needed to be scheduled for surgery *immediately*.

I promptly contacted the *real* experts.

I called the Jewel Stein Eye Institute in Los Angeles for a second opinion referral. The clinic gave me the number of a pediatric ophthalmologist who examined Hannah and began treatment by explaining her condition in detail. Then she did something extraordinary; she required my husband and I to partner with her in the care of our daughter. *Cooperative medicine? What a concept.*

Two years later Hannah did have to have surgery, but her doctor assured me that without all those hours of eye patching and encouragement, Hannah without doubt, would have had to endure more than one surgery to correct the effect of surgery done too soon.

With the storytelling coming to a close, I ask the parents to consider the parallel. I remind them that I value expertise, but encourage them to remember that they alone hold the PhD when it comes to unlocking their child's individuality.

I challenge them to examine the limits of the system and offer them an alternative.

I encourage them that together we will tackle the work of untangling the knotted mass that forced them to dial my number in the first place.

I launch from here into an investigation, "Who is your child?" and the work of awakening genius begins.

FOUR / *Curiouser and Curiouser*

What if our education system were modeled after an artisan guild? Imagine, each student being provided the longitudinal canvas of time during the course of his or her education to engage in the deep practice that establishes habits of being. What if every student were apprenticed in the skills necessary to bloom individuality?

Sadly, an audience with Spielberg, let alone an apprenticeship, is hard to come by these days. But a *virtual apprenticeship*, well this is in the realm of reality.

Alice became "curiouser and curiouser"[29] wandering in Wonderland. Alice is an ideal student. She takes risks, endures humiliation, asks questions, seeks logic, and in the end gains wisdom that she passes on to readers. Story has the power to instruct, rouse, and transform if we dare to dig deep. The Duchess sums things up rather well, "Everything's got a moral, if only you can find it".[50] If our lives are to have purpose, we must press into the process of becoming abundantly ourselves. Yet, there is no number large enough to mirror the times per day that I hear my students say, "I can't." I model my response after the best teacher I've ever met, The White Queen, "I dare say you haven't had much practice," said the Queen. "When I was younger, I always did it for half an hour a day. Why, sometimes I've believed as many as six impossible things before breakfast".[30] Science has long valued curiosity. It's time for education to follow suit. A quality education has everything to do with the cultivation of curiosity, but curiosity needs fertile soil to survive, needs coaxing, and encouragement.

Curiosity breeds imagination, fuels dreams, shapes individuality, and rouses genius.

I have seen students engage in creative endeavors that, over time, allow them to acquire skills that transfer to all subject areas. For this reason we need to act on Robinson's challenge:

> ...the arts, sciences, humanities, physical education, languages, and math all have equal and central contributions to make to a student's education.[31]

The study of creativity—mathematical creativity, musical creativity, visual creativity, scientific creativity and so on—introduces the student to processes and skills necessary to ignite and utilize imagination. Like the White Queen, my job, as an educator is to nourish, inspire, and encourage academic excellence by providing the conditions in which the student's curiosity will thrive.

Children will embrace education—will become students—as they are encouraged to imagine possibility and to enjoy the pursuit of knowledge. Curiosity and imagination are vital to the emotional, intellectual, and spiritual well-being of the child. Stimulating the heart, mind, and soul is essential to a full academic experience, is essential to the cultivation of the individual child.

So what is a virtual mentor and how do we sign them on?

In my school, fall is *Person I Admire* season. This activity, culminating in an oral presentation in costume from the point of view of a famous person, was originally devised as an activity to get my students to read a book. The concept is not revolutionary, no doubt students in a vast range of classrooms across America at one point or another in their schooling have participated in an activity of this nature. But something tremendous happens when students expect this activity each year, same time, same place, when students begin to extend their research for months and beyond. This year we had an anniversary: five students had participated in *Person I Admire* once a year for ten years.

I gave each of these students a few minutes before the presentations began to reminisce and to tell the group what they discovered personally significant. Listening, I realized that this activity had evolved into much more than a clever way to get my students to read. These students were connecting with imagination.

I will never forget the year that my oldest son, now a ten year *Person I Admire* veteran, declared that he wanted to research Frank Gehry. There was no doubt in my mind what had inspired him. His weekly music lessons take place across the street from what was, back then, the construction site of Frank Gehry's LA masterpiece, Walt Disney Concert Hall. So Taylor read books (over and over and over again), visited a local museum exhibit (numerous times) and spent hours in the hands-on architectural activity room designed for children. We even went on a driving tour to see other buildings designed by Frank Gehry in Los Angeles.

Eventually, architectural sculptures began cropping up all over the house—a veritable metropolis in my living room. The application of learning was alive and well. The ultimate fruit of my son's research, research that went on for three years, was to culminate in October of 2003 with the public unveiling of the concert hall.

Taylor at the Walt Disney Concert Hall

Climbing the stairs a few paces ahead of me, donning his idea of the perfect costume, Gehry's concert hall in the form of an enormous hat, my son was deaf to the buzz of astonished whispers swirling. Surveying the lay of the land, connecting one by one with the massive shapes, he was unaware that his presence detracted attention from the inauguration of the icon itself.

While gazing at the shimmering mosaic rose pool, a couple shaking their heads in amusement, walked right up to my little boy and invited him to be part of their photo, a photo I was asked to snap. As quick as the fascinated strangers wrapped their arms around my son's small shoulders the shutter clicked. Handing the camera back to a man I'll never see again, he flashed me a grin and thanked me for the experience. I followed silently two steps behind my son chasing sunlight on stainless steel.

Another man approached the hat only to discover, eyes dropping, that it rested on the head of a small boy. Introducing himself to my son as an award-winning architect, he listened intently to the tale of the hat. Head shaking, eyes twinkling, he patted my son's back, and looked to the sky in wonderment. In the end he asked for my son's name and promised to commit it to memory, "I'll be watching for you Taylor."

Then came a barrage of curious strangers—a tour bus of people snapping pictures like paparazzi of the boy and his hat, fascinated parents demanding the name of my son's teacher, students, security guards, and weary teachers wanting this formula for success. Each managed a moment with my boy and his great silver-winged hat. Taylor gladly shared the story of watching the icon slowly come to life, of the man named Frank O. Gehry who made buildings inspired by fish, and of his own research project that sparked the idea for the hat that triggered all the storytelling in the first place.

Swarms of people came to experience an architectural inauguration and were captivated by something they had not anticipated— a boy wearing a monumental hat. Toward the end of our visit, as I stood beside Gehry's swooping silver sculpture pondering my son's interactions with perfect strangers, a man touched my shoulder and looked intently into my eyes, "You must be doing something right if your kid is into Gehry."

The hat

I realized in that moment that these strangers were reaching out to touch imagination in a bland world. Crossing paths with this child, who connected with creativity and engaged in the work necessary to bring an imagination into reality, forced these strangers to step outside of what they believed a child is capable of and jolted their stereotype. We live in a world where procrastination puts our dreams off until tomorrow and perfectionism keeps our dreams beyond arm's length. I was in the midst of a slice of humanity that had journeyed afar to identify with a stainless steel exclamation point. It struck me that creativity inspires humanity to risk.

Creativity, whatever the form, begs its audience to attend to our longing to eradicate a haunting sense of disconnection. People had come in droves to celebrate face-to-face with Frank Gehry's imagination, had come to prove that outrageous dreams are possible. Gehry's architectural masterpiece begs the question, "Why do we hide in dimly lit boxes behind blinds that keep us safely isolated from the risk of imagination?" His soaring structure presents a challenge to chase away the complacency that isolates humanity. My son, wearing a hat inspired by an architect he has never met, opened the door of imagination for people he will likely never meet again. His hat drew connections like a magnet, broke down walls, and briefly caused lives to intersect in a way that is noteworthy. My son audaciously locking arms with Gehry implored, "Look, me too!" Like Gehry before him, Taylor responded to the creative impulse, opened the blinds, and let the real thing in.

How many hours per day is spent drilling common knowledge into our children? Two? Three hours a day? How many hours do we carve out of the schedule for curiosity?

Exploring imagination will produce students with an enthusiasm and a passion for learning. But when the teacher's hands are tied, the child is consequently unable to attend to developing the critical creative thinking skills that will promote active learning. As educators, we must recognize the role imagination plays in strengthening these skills. Still, the question remains: Where do we find mentors and how do we encourage students to routinely engage with imagination on this level in a society where the concept of artisan guilds has long disappeared? When we begin our lessons with a topic that sparks the student's imagination, as was the case with Taylor's research of Frank Gehry, we are introducing them to a virtual mentor and open the door to limitless opportunities to connect with creative significance.

One of my prized possessions is a folded mass of faded-yellow legal pad with Sara's profuse notes smiling back at me. I was taken back to the summer of 1997. Long before the school, my dear friend and fellow visionary, Sara, and I partnered to create a rich environment for our own children plus a handful of others, in my living room. Our primary goal was to instill a passion for learning that would coax the inner genius into the light. But we faced the age-old dilemma: Who has the resources for one-on-one mentors? So we set our minds to troubleshooting and the concept of the virtual mentor in the classroom was born. Who needs a time machine?

Our goal was to inspire our young girls, then first and third graders, to follow the thread of perseverance to its logical conclusion. We would teach our girls the skill of longitudinal research. So Sara and I headed to my kitchen and began chattering away, brainstorming really, something like this: "What if they engage in research of famous women from history who will model the skill? What if we use great picture books and incorporate sophisticated art materials? Yes! And of course it will be great fun! And, think about it, I mean, we will be exploring literature, and this is history too, right? Ah, the glory of cross-curricular activities!"

So, with a baby on my hip, simultaneously stirring up dinner in a pot on the stove, I imagined with Sara who was, as usual, gripping a yellow legal pad scribbling furiously. By the time we were ready to dish up dinner she had scribbled a dozen pages chock full of ideas to get our girls started. We constructed a series of research questions that the girls would use to guide their year-long research and developed a presentation format. We decided that for each book read, our girls would write a report and craft a creative project depicting the famous woman being researched.

There is something fantastic that happens when we teach students to engage in research over time, when we teach them to value the process of purposeful work that is not instantaneous. Longitudinal research develops the muscle necessary for independent discovery, and I believe it is precisely this type of discovery that leads to the development of critical creative thinking, that mysterious something common to the genius.

The trick to this kind of research is to be prepared. Because we had a plan, we were able to sit with our girls, take turns reading aloud with them, and guide them as they developed the skill of gathering just the right tidbits to include in their simple research paper. We had time to help them explore art materials such as paint and canvas, chalk pastels, and textiles. We were able to encourage Hannah and Evelyn as they endeavored to craft a creative project that would not only celebrate each famous woman but would enable them to recognize the value of seeing a creative work through from the start to the finish line.

Set as a two hour per week activity, generally speaking, we read and wrote about one book per week unless the book was long, in which case this leg of the activity could take a couple of weeks or more (the "there is no hurry" truth applies here), and we completed the artistic activity in two or three weeks. From there, it's all, well, history.

Only looking back do I see the great pay-off, our girls, all grown up, are women who turn heads not only because they are lovely, but because they are busy following threads of perseverance to a logical conclusion. Here are girls who dare to dream and engage in the work of bringing shape to those dreams—geniuses in the making.

> *Q. What sticks with you from your research of Famous Women?*
>
> *A. Hannah: I remember clearly being confused about Polio when we read about Wilma Rudolph, but so impressed that she did not let this mysterious physical handicap stop her from winning gold. I remember making prairie bonnets and dresses when we read about Laura Ingalls Wilder and being thankful that she bothered to share her recollections of pioneer life with me. I remember wishing I could have been a stowaway in that plane with Amelia Earhart and Eleanor Roosevelt. I remember thinking how awful I would have felt in Faith Ringgold's shoes when that teacher told her to give up her dream of becoming an artist because she had no talent... imagine that! Vivid among these memories is having the privilege of meeting Faith Ringgold and being able to share this thought with her in person. I remember making an appliqué wall hanging of Faith Ringgold inspired*

by her many quilt-paintings hanging in museums, like the one I saw at The Metropolitan Museum of Art. I remember my mom reproducing my quilt in miniature so I could cut and paste the images onto greeting cards. I remember handing a stack of these cards tied neatly together with a bow to Faith Ringgold and showing her the quilt I made. I remember that the artist not only autographed my copy of her brand new book, The Invisible Princess, but also applauded my artwork. Research of Famous Women was an ongoing elementary assignment. That was more than ten years ago. After all this remembering, what I remember most is that the assignment still matters.

A. Evelyn: I loved doing art projects to go with our write-ups on each famous woman in history. I clearly remember working on my watercolor of Amelia Earhart one night and showing it off proudly to my brother and his friend. I remember when Hannah and I sat together and traced drawings from the book about Wilma Rudolph and learned about her inspiring story of perseverance. I remember working on my art project for Faith Ringgold—it was a canvas divided into three sections depicting things I love—cooking, my friends, and art—and illustrating scenes that were important in Faith's life. I remember specifically learning about how an art teacher told Faith Ringgold she could never become an artist because she didn't know how to paint mountains. I thought that was so unfair because Faith had never even seen mountains before. Getting to actually meet Faith Ringgold and show her my art project, well, how many kids get that kind of opportunity? I was recently reading my college art appreciation book and I noticed artwork by Ringgold and I said to myself, "I've met her!" I remember learning about the first black woman millionaire, Madam C.J. Walker. I liked learning about how she created beauty products for women. Entrepreneurial success stories have fascinated me ever since. I remember painting a portrait of Princess Diana and on "Person I Admire Day" dressing up like her. One not so fond memory is when I spent what seemed like hours crafting my write up on Louisa May Alcott and then accidentally feeding it through our paper shredder! These things happen! When we read about Rachel Carson, we participated in a coastal cleanup day. I still carry with me striking memories from our research and art projects.

Hannah and Evelyn
on Laura Ingalls-Wilder's porch, Mansfield , Missouri

Amelia Earhart
cardboard assemblage,
chalk pastel and buttermilk

Eleanor Roosevelt
acrylic on canvas

Wilma Rudolph
acrylic on canvas and
watercolor collage

I have a magnet collection on the inside of our medicine cabinet so we can dream big while we brush our teeth. My favorite is a Leonardo da Vinci quote "Art is never finished, only abandoned."

So what has art to do with the state of education in America? Everything. We need to move beyond the workforce preparation model and address the deeper individual needs that are ignored in mass education. How can we provide opportunities for our children to develop critical creative thinking skills?

Leonardo da Vinci left us tremendous insight into his work habits. He painstakingly collected thousands of his ideas in sketchbooks, most of which would never be fully realized. But I'll venture to say there is not one who would dare call him a slacker. There are academic skills that do not fall under the Three Rs umbrella.

When my daughter Hannah was 10 she began tackling Debussy's *Doctor Gradus ad Parnassum* on the piano. I was scrubbing pots and pans in the kitchen, listening as she delicately worked through each new section. Because I was not intimately familiar with the piece back then, I called out, "Is that the Debussy?"

"No, this is mine."

I dropped the pot back into sudsy water, quickly wiped my hands, and walked to the piano, "Your piece?"

"Yes."

"Play it for me..." and she did, jubilantly, without hesitation. Hannah was composing.

When she turned 13, things began to change. She began to depend on notes more than her ear. Concurrent with her sight-reading ability jumping a few notches, she became insecure with her creative voice. No amount of coaxing would console the teenage composer to come out of hiding. She wanted to create, but in her mind her ideas never sounded just right. Hannah became paralyzed by perfectionism.

Over the course of the next few years I presented opportunities and encouraged her to engage in the process of creating. I reminded Hannah that creating something happens with little steps that begin with an idea, "Remember, good old Da Vinci said, 'Art is never finished only abandoned'."

Fast forward, three years ago an 18-year-old Hannah composed a piece for piano and charanga that involved more conversation, more tears, and more hugs than hands on the keys and pencil to staff paper. The fact that the project was to be submitted for a competition made the work real but ultimately Hannah's prize was persevering through the process of developing an idea, even if the idea failed.

I will never forget her beaming smile the day we played back the final mixed recording of "Empty Halls." The composition did not win a prize in the competition that year, but did receive encouraging notes back from the adjudicators. The notes were more valuable to Hannah than a cash prize. "Empty Halls" whispers to this day, "Keep working at your craft, you are a composer."

A year later, Evelyn, was collaborating with my son, Taylor, on a film they were to submit to a competition and asked Hannah permission to use *Empty Halls* as the music for the film. She granted permission. The film won regional recognition in the Scholastic Arts and Writing Awards competition.

This past year, Hannah composed a film score for a competition sponsored by the Music Teacher's Association of California. There were a few bumpy, tear-filled stretches, but she persevered through the creative process with very little coaching. Hannah's film score won first place in her division.

Yesterday my 21-year-old daughter came home from a day of practicing music and handed me her cell phone to listen to a sketch she recorded, "I started a new composition."

"An abandoned idea?"

"Yes, tear free."

Empty Halls

from Amphidromic Point

(http://bit.ly/Empty-Halls)

I've come to realize that the virtual mentor is only part of the battle. Carving time for students to explore and discover the limits of their imagination in response to their mentor's lesson leads to a plethora of critical creative thinking.

Bingo ball O 74

With a bingo ball and a Lego block, that's how it always begins.

It is a typical shopping day: Hop in the car. Back out of the driveway. "Who has the list?" Oops... forgot the list, back into the driveway. Søren is chosen for the journey there and back again. I watch him up the driveway... there he goes, two minutes later he's back again clutching the list triumphantly. My youngest son jumps into the car and we're off...

We arrive at Trader Joe's in nothing flat. In summer we don't have to battle traffic patterns. Splitting the list into five sections, we scurry in five directions, grab the goods and get in line. It's a little game we play, our version of *Beat the Clock*. I get a kick out of the items slipped into the cart by my frenetic shoppers: Crispy Crunchy Chocolate Chip Cookies, Altoids, frozen pizza, Hansen's Soda, lime popsicles, and even rice milk when they're desperate. Sometimes I smile, let them see me turn a blind eye, but mostly I draw the line, "Put it back please."

On this particular day, the first shopping day of summer, we are fast, no doubt accomplishing our trip in record time. The five of us want nothing more than to be home doing nothing, that's right *n-o-t-h-i-n-g*.

When we arrive home, the finely tuned chaotic task of carrying in and putting away the groceries begins. We drop the bags as close to the back door as possible. Then my three sons throw the contents one by one in rapid fire to Hannah who is waiting by the open refrigerator door. I usually head outside about this time on the pretense of double-checking the car, *"Wouldn't want to forget that bag with the ice cream."* In reality, I'm avoiding the flying carton of eggs, slowly counting backwards from ten.

Three or four steps later I recognize a familiar sight: the hatch is open, the car doors too, so I peek in and there it is, sneering up at me: Bingo ball O 74.

I pick up the evidence, tuck it into my pocket, and begin preparing for the deposition: *"Please respond to Exhibit A..."*

Surprisingly, I remain patient. Despite the fact that little lost game pieces and Lego blocks startle my bare feet in the middle of the night. As I walk into the kitchen (by now the celery's flying), I see my four enjoying the work of being a family. I remind myself that someday I might actually miss primary red, yellow, and blue Legos sneering, "*We got you!*" on my midnight path.

In the end I simply tap my eldest son, Taylor, on the shoulder and hold out my open palm cradling O 74, "Would you mind putting this away?"

Later that night, when I reach for a book atop the piano, a bothersome sight catches my eye... "Oh *Taylor*..."

"Yes mom?"

"Didn't I ask you to put this away earlier?"

"Yes... but I made a sculpture."

"A sculpture?

"I call it *'Bingo Ball and a Lego Piece'*."

Promoting creative thinking is not simply a matter of encouragement. The mentor must also recognize the child's creative efforts as intellectually valuable, so much more than child's play that must be cleaned up at the end of the day.

I remember entering the last leg of my MFA journey. During my residency, each day I left the house with complete confidence—I had to—that my three sons were safe under the supervision of their sister, 20-year-old-benevolent-dictator, Hannah. But when she picked me up each day at 6, I braced myself for the debriefing of the day's adventure by all four of my children, which began a simultaneous broadcast as soon as the seatbelt clicked:

> *Liam wanted me to drive through the carwash*
>
> *and Hannah blasted the theme song to Little Big Planet,*
>
> *...at the park, there was a... rode my scooter and fed the ducks...*

> *library and Barnes and Noble there was a book with a Lego guy*
>
> *and I checked out a book about orchestration so I can...*
>
> *one on Constantine's early rule and a biography of John Lennon...*

Surveying the state of the house when I arrive home, I realize the morning was an equal bundle of good times. I begin to tidy the clues. I don't mind the mess. The process of cleaning up actually helps me unwind after a day of academia... I mean *literally unwind.*

I follow a mass of tangled white yarn that is strewn from the kitchen to the living room. What I discover at the end of the line is tremendous—two forks cocooned to stillness, functional objects transformed to a beautifully still, nonfunctional state. I pause in awe of the ingenuity that drove the artist into this work and marvel at the result. The sculpture speaks to me, begs a question, "Is the yarn limiting the fork or expanding its potential?"

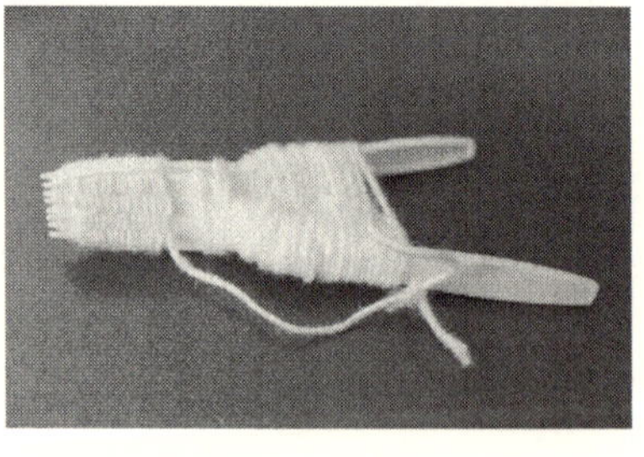

Fork + yarn

I collect the fork sculpture and head toward the *Gathering Ledge,* the place in my kitchen where I put such misfit items, and kneel to my hands and knees to begin scooping loose items from the floor. I pick up some stray pencils, toy cars, and sit up when I come upon two sheets of paper, ovals mysteriously cut out of the center.

Back on my feet, I move swiftly toward the trash and am halted when my peripheral vision is intrigued by a yellow blur... *the missing ovals.* But they are much more than ovals. They are *prototypes,* furniture design—a bench and a chair that would make Charles and Ray Eames proud.

Folding chair

Not sure where I collected the *Eye* that's painted on a scrap of canvas, but I do know that Taylor plans for this to be a small contribution to a very large installation.

Finally I scoop up two phone books, the *Yellow Pages,* the ones that Hannah and Taylor have big plans for, a top-secret video project (shhhhhh...). I set the books on the ledge with *Forks Woven to One by Yarn, Oval Prototypes of a Bench and a Chair, Eye* and *Bingo Ball and Lego Block.*

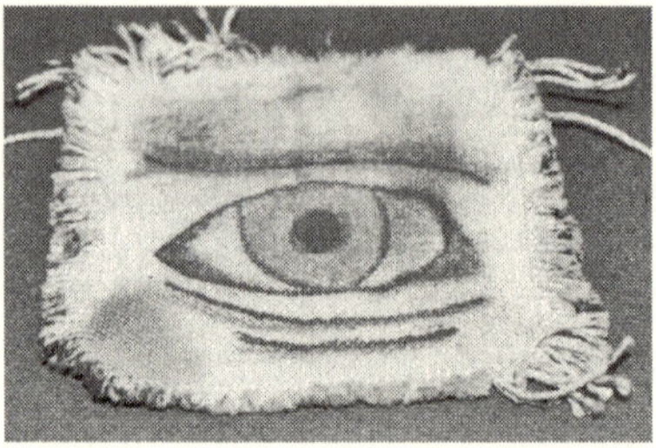

Canvas eye

At the end of my tidying, I survey the items perched on the *Gathering Ledge* and sense a connection sparking.

Last week Sunday, was the close of *Leonardo Da Vinci and the Art of Sculpture: Inspiration and Invention*. We made the trip up to the exhibit twice and pulling into the parking structure for a third visit. I was glad.

Inside the gallery, Taylor taps me on the shoulder, "Look at *this* Mom! On the same page, the face of Dante and the design for a mechanical military device."

I nod speechlessly.

We move around the gallery packed with voracious viewers on this closing day of the exhibit, overwhelmed by page after page, a royal sampling of Da Vinci's sketchbooks (many belonging to Queen Elizabeth II), pages we will most likely never seen again.

Hannah waves to me. She is intrigued by a page that began with a sketch executed by one of Leonardo's students. Apparently a portion of the sketch, the right arm gesture, was not up to Leonardo's standards. Leonardo corrected the problem with a single line. But the correction seemed to send Da Vinci on a stream-of-consciousness exploration because the page was a mass of perfect scribbles. He frenetically drew horses in various rearing positions plus several designs for military weapons and machinery. She looks at the page and shakes her head in amazement.

"I know," I say, "Can't you just imagine the wide-eyed student silently slipping away from the lesson while Da Vinci slipped into a creative stupor?"

Looking around, I realize that most of what I am able to absorb is unfinished, unrealized. Does this make Leonardo a slacker? ...*I wouldn't dare.* In that moment Leonardo da Vinci became *my* virtual mentor.

Back home I take a second look at my *Gathering Ledge,* superimpose what I see on my memory of the Getty exhibit and have proof positive: I am in the midst of genius.

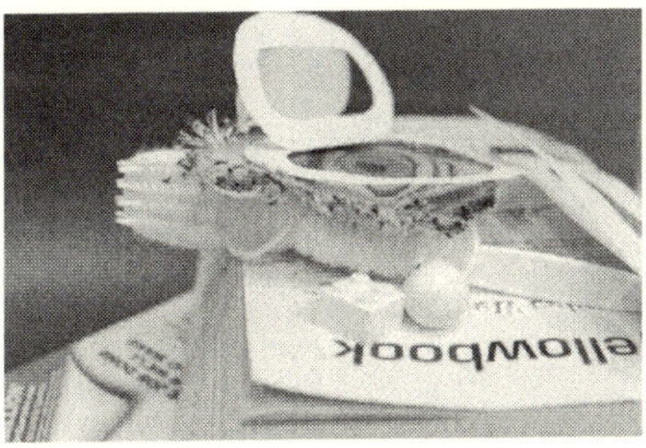

The Gathering Ledge

On the way home I purposed to grow that ledge, purposed to give my children more room to explore the process of being creative, *more Da Vinci moments.* There is no space for perfection on the *Gathering Ledge*, only space for burgeoning imagination. And procrastination? Well, that end of the spectrum collects a different kind of dust.

Weeks into the Leonardo da Vinci experiment, I woke up to another creative endeavor in progress. Let's just say that Taylor began sketching with a phone book. He pushed furniture aside and turned his loft wall space into his temporary canvas. And the result is another reminder that boys (and girls) need space to explore their imagination.

Yellow pages

And this just in, the eye on canvas became part of a larger project. I think it is important to note that Taylor won a Regional Silver Key from the Scholastic Arts & Writing Awards in 2011 for his multi-media composition, "Saving Face."

Saving Face

I was alone with my youngest son, Søren, on a blustery Wednesday. All is cozy until I noticed the symptoms of boredom surfacing. Honestly, I was hoping that Søren's imagination would entertain him so that I could tackle my never-ending stacks of work, but soon realized this was selfish, another instance of my taking his creativity and contemplative nature for granted.

Inking

I've tried linoleum with young children with little success because the medium demands a significant degree of fine motor control. Nowadays, making a relief block print is much easier because the carving is done on a material more like a plastic eraser. So I got my son started, hovering close by to direct him, as needed, through all the stages of the process. Søren worked happily for three hours straight drawing, carving, inking, printing... even cleaning up!

Pressing

I could have coaxed my son toward independent play, but I read a book on the treadmill recently about happiness that reminded me, "Most people do not regularly ask, 'Will this make me happier?' before engaging in some action. Rather, they do what they do because it feels good at the moment".[32]

The print

I want my artistic Søren to have the ability to make choices that will promote his curious nature. Right now my job as his mother-mentor is to help him fill his toolbox with possibility.

FIVE / *Straw to Gold*

Everyone wants to spin straw to gold.

Alchemy.

When the king locked the farmer's daughter in that tower with a haystack and demanded gold, she wept. It wasn't until Rumpelstiltskin entered the scene that her hope was reanimated. But it was the protagonist's risky action—the offering of something precious to that mad little gnome of a man—that ultimately spun the girl's straw to gold.

When children are taught to believe that imagination is not frivolous, they become alchemists.

When it comes to the way we approach the education of our children, let's face it: the sky *is* falling. But I believe we can put it right if we dare to awaken the slumbering genius, one individual at a time. We need to re-imagine educational outcomes. Don't we want education to provide opportunities for our children to breathe and to explore the wide-open spaces of possibility? We must carve time for curiosity. Education must be about protecting and promoting individuality at all costs.

Kingfisher,
Hannah, age 14
after Van Gogh

Arles, 9 April 1888, Vincent Van Gogh to his dear Theo:

> You can't be at the pole and the equator at the same time. You must choose your own line, as I hope to do, and it will probably be colour.[33]

I always run through my lesson beforehand. Tomorrow a dozen apprentices will study Van Gogh's canvas with me.

I'll begin with an introduction:

> *There are three primary colors, red, yellow, and blue. From these colors, orange, green, and violet are born. Add the tertiary list – red-violet/red-orange, yellow-orange / yellow-green, blue-green / blue-violet – and you have yourself a complete wheel.*

Not only are we dealing with chemistry and physics, the science of color is magical. Add black and white into the mix and the whole thing is out of control.

> *There are infinite greens for a painter to explore.*

I will let my knife cut into ropes of paint, demonstrate how to conjure a hue.

> *These are the blue-greens, there are no cool blues—no cobalt, no ultramarine. The greens in this painting are blue warmed by yellow—turquoise deep, transparent viridian—lightened up with unbleached titanium. Maybe a bit of sap green too, certainly never straight from the tube. And do you see how the painter used a bit of vermilion for zing?*
>
> *Van Gogh painted his greens fearlessly, undiluted, windy, sun-drenched.*

All the while, I will be folding pigment on my palette.

> *When it comes to mixing greens, not all blues and yellows are equal.*

Preparing for tomorrow, I discover in "The Kingfisher," a mass of yellow—greens with a touch of red—orange, blue—greens with a touch of yellow-orange. I sense the palette knife slipping through pigment scraping glass as I prepare the palette for tomorrow. I will remind them:

His color is hyperbolic, his strokes aggressive. And it is important to note that a stuffed bird inspired the subject of the painting.

Was Van Gogh performing some kind of CPR?

I am ready now. I tuck all the greens in airtight containers, gather my brushes, canvas, and pack the supplies into my car for tomorrow's lesson.

In the morning, backing out of the driveway, I hear a loud crack and panic. Only a tree branch, phew. I hop back into the car, peer twice in the rearview mirror before proceeding, all clear. But in that moment I pause to catch a glimpse of the past.

Is this foreshadowing in reverse?

Seven years ago, back when the classroom guild was still in my living room, I heard the sound of a branch cracking.

I'm an educator, a poet, a visual artist who is often met with a blank stare when I mention that my career is rooted in the home school community; a stare that is Siamese twin to a patronizing nod. Let's just say that the path I find myself on is not well worn. I have bramble scars to prove it.

So seven years ago, ah yes...

My neighbor was a public school teacher who, like Gladys Kravitz, from Bewitched, with her worn spiral notebook in hand wondered what in the world was going on in her neighborhood. What kind of people homeschool their children? A dozen parents lined up to drop their children off at 9 and scoop them up at 3 is an expected sight at any local school, but not at the foot of a rural neighborhood driveway.

Eventually she knocked on my door, "We've tried everything else."

I agreed to bring her at-risk son into our guild. "He can join our literature circle, our writing, and art workshops. I'll check on his progress in math, science, and history at noon on Wednesdays."

I am sure this mother loves her son, but she was critical, "Smart-as-a-whip lazy," she would say as the boy's eyes pleaded with me to help her understand. This was a bright boy.

One Wednesday, well into our established routine, I walked out my front door and was met by an annoying screech. Tree trimming. When I smelled eucalyptus mourning its fate, I paused to stare at the hewn limbs strewn in queue near the chipper.

I felt a metaphor emerging.

One branch in particular was whispering a final plea, "Save me."

In the time it took me to walk across the street on my way to the tutoring session, it's beautiful green—the specific hue that makes Eucalyptus, Eucalyptus—was shredded to gray in the chipper.

With my eye back in the present, I peer into my rearview mirror and I wonder, "Has that mother's son become what she imagined, smart-as-a-whip lazy, has he been crushed by the most frightening chipper of all?"

Sadly this boy did not have the opportunity to explore his individuality in the classroom guild for long. His mother eventually decided to relocate closer to her extended family. I believed in this boy's genius, but back then he was spending his emotional energy on emotional survival. His father abandoning the family left this boy empty and angry. This mother was spent. This boy was spent. There was nothing left for establishing habits of being.

Some things in life are beyond the scope of education.

Here and now, seven years later, on my way to mentor a group of students as they explore the greens of Van Gogh's palette, the crack of a branch beneath my tires reminds me to keep this metaphor in mind and the iPod shuffles Kasabian's "Where Did All the Love Go". May be a misreading, but taking the lyrics at face value,

"My sentiment exactly."

Van Gogh's furious strokes will roll down my cheeks as I implore my apprentices to join the painter who perched his green for all the world to see. I hand them their brushes so they, too, might paint their dreams impasto, "Living Green for the Kingfisher."

Recently my friend Lori and I sat down to tea to debrief on the week's events. Lori is Montessori trained and a passionate history teacher. She began to relay a haunting scene:

I was talking with a friend about books when a co-worker, an exceptional young man in his twenties, chimed in, "How many books have you read?

I looked at him, "Well, what do you mean? This week? This month?"

"No, how many books have you read in your lifetime?"

I shot him a puzzled glance, "Well... thousands."

"Really?"

"Why do you ask?"

"I was just listening to you talk so enthusiastically and was curious. Thing is, well, I bet I've read under 10 books in my life."

On the way home my iPod shuffles again, this time it is Mumford and Sons crooning "The Cave" making sure I remember that the desire to become settled in our individuality is universal, not just an educational void.

These scenarios are an ever-increasing norm.

What pricked Lori's heart is that this young man actually felt bad about the fact that he never acquired the habit of reading. Here is a man who is curious about books, but hasn't a clue where to begin.

The problem we face is not about reading.

We need to reach into culture, have-a-look-see. Just as literacy is so much more than the ability to read, creativity is so much more than the arts. An archaic model of education devoid of creativity is thwarting individuality.

When students aren't taught to listen for and respond to their creative impulse, their curiosity dwindles.

The absence of curiosity is tragic.

This is Van Gogh's "The Exercise Yard" and we are standing in the gallery watching all those prisoners carve a circular rut while the moths fluttering above their heads point to the one way out.

Active learning is hope.

Active learning involves work and, as educators, we have the singular responsibility to make that work personally meaningful for the sake of the individual.

* * *

In March of 2005, I got a call from my sister-in-law who had tickets to one of the opening shows of U2's, Vertigo tour. It was late notice, but did Willie and I want to go to the show?

"Um, yes." So they picked us up an hour later and we headed to San Diego.

Henri Matisse reminds us:

> A painter doesn't see everything he has put in his paintings. It is other people who find these treasures in it, one by one, and the richer the painting is in surprises of this sort, in treasures, the greater the author.[34]

I never have been one to take anything at face value, so I began watching, reaching for significance in this spontaneous event. By the time we got to the stadium, people were in queue. I made an immediate association between this and my array of experience with the exhibitions of Van Gogh's work. I thought of Dorothea Lange's Depression Era photographs.

This was a bread line.

People were hungry and U2 was offering crumbs.

Our tickets in the nosebleed section were the best seats in the house for this poet. I translated the scene to poem on a scrap of paper during our drive back to Los Angeles after the concert:

'40' reprise

Inspiration: San Diego, CA 2005

"It's goin' off in the heart!"

An audacious voice reverberates
Pelting insatiable stones with the real thing
As three spur him on:

"We hurt each other and we do it again

... love, the higher law
One life you get to do what you should
One life with each other,
My Sisters, my brothers

Hear her coming, Lord
Hear us call
Hear us knocking
We're knocking at your door
Hear us coming, Lord
Hear us call
Hear us scratching
Pleading: Let us crawl!"

15,000 drunken souls wail:
How long to sing this song?
How long to sing this song?
How long to sing this song?

On and on and on
They plead until houselights
Silence their psalm

His Holy Spirit murmurs
Stillness throughout the stadium
Our hearts are pierced
And Richter spikes to Heaven

The very next morning, the press was abuzz:

> And what made its final encore so memorable Monday at the ipayOne Center was that the sold-out audience of 14,500, not the four-man Irish band, performed the final refrain of "40." And that concluded the opening night of U2's "Vertigo/2005" world tour, at what was formerly the San Diego Sports Arena.

> A stirring song of unity, redemption and divine inspiration based on Psalm 40 from the Bible, "40" dates back 22 years to the band's third album, "War." Or as Bono, U2's iconic singer, told the cheering crowd: "We haven't played this one since 1983," when it was a staple of the group's sets. One by one, band members exited the stage, leaving drummer Larry Mullen Jr. to lay down a snappy backbeat as the audience sang the refrain of "40": How long to sing this song? When he, too, left the stage, the audience continued singing, a cappella, even after the house lights came up.[35]

Later that year, I carried the poem to NYC, had it in my pocket to remind my eyes to pay close attention while I swallowed more U2 crumbs at Madison Square Garden. I was haunted by that initial experience in San Diego.

When Tracey told me that she was taking Brian to another U2 concert for his birthday, this time in Los Angeles, I folded my poem for her pocket, just in case. Funny thing is, seems their pit tickets were golden and admitted them into the inner circle. They made their way to the front and when Bono reached out his hand to my-sister-in-law during the last song, she reached into her pocket and slipped him my poem. Quick thinking!

The end of the story goes something like this: When U2 came back out for the encore, Bono looked for Tracey, tapped his heart, a gesture of thanks.

That year, that particular album, *How to Dismantle an Atomic Bomb,* was intriguing, relevant—political, emotional, and spiritual. Bono became my virtual mentor. One song in particular captured my imagination: "Sometimes You Can't

Make it on Your Own." Bono was grieving his father's death and graciously invited us to be a fly on the wall. I watched the interviews. I read the book.

> I found a rusty nail...'You look at it, you stare at it and go: 'Wow. I didn't know that it was there.' Then you put it back in the glass of water. [laughs] The only difference is now you know it's there and the water's been disturbed and discolored. But you didn't take it out and get rid of it. So I think if you're gonna listen to yourself in these moments, and you discover stuff about yourself that you don't like, that you have a duty to fix them. Because if you don't, then it's either the thing that I said earlier the 'pickled' thing, where there is self-indulgence, or you just end up disturbing the waters, and it doesn't lead you anywhere.[36]

But it was the music video for that song that put his words into action—Bono removing a rusty nail from his jar. My life has been one atomic bomb after another. Bono taught me to grieve. He ran his gauntlet over and over, facing his grief alone, but all the while his community—Edge, Larry, and Adam—were playing back-up. Sometimes you can't make it on your own.

Some days I feel I'm fifteen meters away from the front line, barefoot on a European battlefield beside spectres of world war, the baffled commander shouting, "Fire at will!" I'm knee-deep in sand weeping, as rusting stones scour a stained shore. Here in the 21st century, I'm wandering stunned in a sanitized version of invasion, far from

Normandy as Costco shoppers fill monster-sized carts with remedies to soothe their oozing wounds. I'm stuck in a line with corpses moaning, threading the loop at Starbucks.

The creative impulse is sparked in chaotic moments such as these.

Creativity is forged out of disorder, is the process that brings shape to an idea trapped in chaos.

It seems to me that banishing chaos from the classroom diminishes this type of experience.

The creative impulse is the catalyst that prods me to actively respond, to engage with the chaotic world.

Chaos is not to be feared.

Chaos must be harnessed.

Creativity helps me process what I encounter in the world and orders the chaos swirling around me. The creative impulse is the catalyst that prods me to engage with the world. Defining precisely how I respond to that creative impulse is a complex process, described to a T in Art and Fear:

> ...like Dorothy trying to describe the land of Oz to Auntie Em. Between the initial idea and the finished piece lies a gulf we can see across, but never fully chart.[37]

When I apply my knowledge of the creative process to educating the child, one thing I know for sure, the only way for students to learn to listen for and respond to the creative impulse is to provide opportunity after opportunity for them to try. They will both fail and succeed. Both are valuable.

I am making sense of the 21st century through the connections I make with the past, endeavoring to help my students do the same. So, machete in hand, I spend my days leading expeditions of students into the unknown territory following the footsteps of creators gone before us. I teach them, as Picasso, to eavesdrop on the creative process:

> You should constantly try to paint like someone else. But the thing is you can't! You should like to. You try. But it turns out to be a botch... And it is at the very moment you make a botch of it that you're yourself.[38]

There is nothing new under the sun, but I've discovered that wandering with the muse in a crevice of history is just the thing that releases the stuff that poems and paintings and musical compositions are made of. Paul Johnson's examination of the creative process, *Creators,* is an excellent guild resource. He reminds us that there is relevancy waiting to be extracted from the body of work left to us by artists of the past,

> All creative individuals build on the works of their predecessors. No one creates in vacuo. All civilizations evolve from earlier societies.[39]

Critical creative thinking enables the individual to abandon the distractions of the immediate and to engage in the work of shaping an idea. And it is this abandonment that brings shape to the individual.

Responding to the creative impulse is a singularly individual responsibility. The individual must do the work of exploring individuality, but the community must promote that work in the first place. I've adopted the World War II motto of the 506th Infantry Regiment of the 101st Airborne Division. I challenge students of all ages to shout, "Currahee!" *Stand alone together.* I encourage them to engage in the work of creativity, to bask in the wisdom from which the motto stems. In the classroom, my students are a band of brothers.

I have listened to children and adults alike who have great ideas.

Great ideas stirring...

So what stops us from chasing our dreams?

Perfectionism?

Procrastination?

Each child has been endowed with the potential to do great things.

My friend Shirean has a son who is a songwriter. As always, I'm pretty sure he didn't craft "To Take on the World" as an anthem to inspire critical creative thinking, but that's precisely how I use this song inside my classroom guild. I agree with Nathan, to take on the world sure would be something.

Active learning is deeply soul satisfying and allows the individual to experience a well of joy. Protecting individuality and promoting critical creative thinking in the classroom guild cultivates sustainable learning. Building habits of this nature—habits of being—are constantly renewed as the student develops.

It is my privilege as a parent and educator to protect and cultivate this potential.

We need to evacuate our children from the low expectations that stem from the self and from culture at large. I will never forget the mother who looked me straight in the eye and thanked me for encouraging her son "who would never amount to much." Then there was the teacher who erased a fourth grade boy's poetic depiction of a struggle between good and evil. As the poet mentor I was shocked, especially in light of the fact that this boy's poem was in conversation with Peter Jackson's film adaptation of Tolkien's Lord of the Rings trilogy. This teacher was so tied to protocol that he didn't recognize the literary and cultural significance of the boy's poetic effort. This student was trying to make sense of his real world by connecting with truth embedded in a story. I tried to reason with the teacher but he insisted the poem be toned down. The boy's re-write was watery and meaningless, completely inauthentic. I can't help but wonder how the experience of having his words erased impacted this child's heart.

The best syllabus in the world—the very best one, the one that includes all the right content—even that syllabus will not in and of itself develop critical creative thinking skills in our children. Being bound to syllabus and content alone is an archaic model, one that consumes precious time and is often irrelevant to individuality.

As an educator, I will continue to inspire as many students as possible to press into their uniqueness by teaching them to elevate their imagination, to generate creative work, and to celebrate being a creator.

Because I'm dedicated to my night job—pressing into protecting and promoting my individuality through my own creative work—I'm empowered to meet the dawn and remind my students that, as individuals we may stand alone, but we stand alone together,

"Currahee!"

works cited

1. Virginia Euwer Wolff. *The Mozart Season* (New York: Square Fish, 2007). 1.

2. Flannery O'Connor. *Everything that Rises Must Converge* (New York: Farrar, Straus, Giroux, 1956). 190.

3. Ken Robinson Ph.D. *Out of our Minds: Learning to be Creative* (West Sussex: Capstone Publishing Limited, 2001). 203.

4. Hanna Volavkova, editor. *I Never Saw Another Butterfly: Children's Drawings and Poems from Terezin Concentration Camp, 1942-1944* (New York: Schocken Books, 1993). 4.

5. Ibid., xx.

6. Elena Makarova. *Friedl Dicker-Brandeis 1898 – 1944*. Jewish Women's Archive. http://jwa.org/encyclopedia/article/dicker-brandeis-friedl

7. Judy Salamon. "Keeping Creativity Alive." New York Times, September 10, 2004. http://www.nytimes.com/2004/09/10/arts/design/10SALA.html

8. Elizabeth Cowling, et al. *Matisse Picasso* (New York: Tate Publishing, 2002). 24.

9. Medeleine, L'Engle. *Walking on Water: Reflections on Faith and Art* (Harold Shaw Publishers, 1980). 79.

10. David Bayles and Ted Orland. *Art and Fear: Observations On The Perils (and Rewards) of Artmaking* (Eugene: Image Continuum Press, 2007). 39..

11. Patricia Polacco. *Appelemando's Dreams* (New York: Putnam Juvenile, 1997) 29.

12. David Mackay Wilson. "Developmentally Appropriate Practice in the Age of Testing." Harvard Education Letter, 25.3 (2009): Web.

March 11, 2011..

13. Leo Lionni. *Frederick* (New York: Scholastic, Inc. , 1967). 18.

14. Vincent Van Gogh. *The Complete Letters of Vincent Van Gogh with Reproductions of All the Drawings in Correspondence* (New York: New York Graphic Society, 1959) 12.

15. Pau; Elie. *The Life You Save May be Your Own: An American Pilgrimage* (New York: Farrar, Straus and Giroux, 2004). x.

16. Ibid., xi.

17. Bayles and Orland, 49..

18. Tennessee Williams. *The Theatre of Tennessee Williams, Volume 1* (New York: New Directions Books, 1971). 18.

19. John Gatto. *Dumbing Us Down.* (Gabriola Island: New Society, 2002). xxxv.

20. K.A. Paris. *A leadership model for planning and implementing change for school-to-work transition.* (Madison: University of Wisconsin-Madison, Center on Education and Work, 1994). 22-25.

21. Melissa Healy. "Beyond the Mozart Effect." The Los Angeles Times, (March 1, 2010). E1.

22. Ibid., E5.

23. Ibid., E5.

24. James Legge. *Confucian Analects.* (Whitefish: Kessinger Publishing, LLC, 2004). 24.

25. L'Engle, 67.

26. Charles Baxter. *Through the Safety Net* (New York: Vintage Books, 1998). 169.

27. Frederick Buechner. *Telling the Truth: The Gospel as Tragedy, Comedy, & Fairy Tale* (San Francisco: Harper San Francisco, 1977). 97.

28. Bruce Cole. *The Renaissance Artist at Work: From Pisano to Titian* (Boulder: Westview Press, 1990). 33

29. Lewis Caroll. *Alice's Advetures in Wonderland and Through the Lokking Glass* (New York: Penguin, 2000). 26.

30. Carroll, 176.

31. Ken Robinson Ph.D.. *The Element: How Finding Your Passion Changes Everything* (New York: Viking, 2009). 247.

32. Dennis Prager. *Happiness is a Serious Problem.* (New York: Harper's Collins Publishers, 1998). 7.

33. Vincent Van Gogh. *The Letters of Vincent Van Gogh* (New York: Penguin Group, 1997). 348.

34. Robinson, "Minds," 9.

35. George Varga. "U2 Opener Uneven Yet Uplifting, Unifying," The Sandego Union Tribune, March 30, 2005: http://www.signonsandiego.com/uniontrib/20050330/news_1c30u2.html.

36. Bayles and Orland, 51.

37. Dore Ashton, ed. *Picasso On Art* (New York: De Capo Press, 1972) 53.

38. Paul Johnson. *Creators.* (New York: HarperCollins Publishers, 2006) 4.

39. Bayles and Orland, 37.

40. Genevieve Morgan. *Matisse: The Artist Speaks* (San Francisco: Collins Publishers, 1996). 61.

41. George Varga. "U2 Opener Uneven Yet Uplifting, Unifying," The Sandego Union Tribune, March 30, 2005: http://www.signonsandiego.com/uniontrib/20050330/news_1c30u2.html

42. Michka Assayas. *Bono in Conversation with Michka Assayas* (New York: Penguin Publishing Group, 2005). 138.

appendix

Snapshots from the Guild

We begin to promote the ecology of individuality as we provide opportunities for students to be mentored by creators who have spent their life building habits of being—habits that, once achieved, are continually renewable. When our students engage with the world swirling about them in meaningful ways, then, and only then, is sustainable learning achieved.

Our goal in the classroom should never be merely content oriented, but rather, the content of the lesson should always play a secondary role to the promotion of individuality and the development of critical creative thinking in each student. The Bauhaus design principle, "form follows function," applies here. In the same way that the architect must consider how a building will be used before designing it, the teacher must consider the individuality of the child and do everything possible to help that individuality coalesce. Moving on from here, we transform the classroom into the *classroom guild* by bridging the gap between simply delivering a lesson and mentoring a child.

When we challenge our students to learn what the likes of a Beatrix Potter or an Albert Einstein accomplished during their life and to keenly observe their complete oeuvre, these great women and men will become the master teachers that mentor our students. This done, we enable students to embrace the habits of being that will lead them to marvel at possibilities.

Following are four examples of virtual mentors invited into my classroom guild and the lessons cajoled from their visits—Pablo Picasso, J.R.R. Tolkien, Lewis Carroll, plus a host of contemporary artists and scientists who are building a bridge between the two disciplines. It is important to recognize that these lessons, though they fall into specific academic categories, are not intended to fulfill an objective on a list of required content. The ultimate goal is always to provide students an opportunity to explore a topic in the classroom guild through which they might grow and be strengthened.

A Day in the Life: Eavesdropping on Picasso and the Artists Influenced by Cubism

Concept and Objectives

Through storytelling, observation, discussion, and research, introduce students to a pocket of virtual collaboration between artists and musicians. As apprentices—5th grade through high school—follow this group of artists and musicians through time to explore the origins and impact of Cubism, they begin to recognize visual art as language.

- Spark the creative impulse
- Promote critical creative thinking in the area of creative writing and visual arts
- Explore the steps involved in the creative process by creating an original poem, short story or visual work

Required Materials

- Simple books about Picasso such as, *Picasso (Getting to Know the World's Greatest Artists)*, by Mike Venezia, or *Famous Artists: Picasso*, by Anthony Mason
- A print or virtual image of Picasso's "Guernica"

Possible Connections To Other Subjects

Following are suggestions for further research:

- Explore the seven quatrains of "Jabberwocky"—sensible nonsense that is Cubist in nature. Lewis Carroll's neologisms, or *portmanteaus*, framed in hyperbolic poetry like a Cubist painting, will make your head spin,

  'Twas brillig, and the slithy toves
  Did gyre and gimble in the wabe:
  All mimsy were the borogoves,
  And the mome raths outgrabe

  –Jabberwocky (excerpt), Lewis Carroll

- Explore the music of Arnold Schonberg who enlisted in Picasso's war. Listen to his twelve-tone compositions and the concept of "emancipated dissonance" to discover the resonating melody beneath the Cubist notes.

Back Story, Lesson, and Charge

Recently I introduced a group of my students to the numerous pockets of creative thought that continue to be sparked by Cubism. I began the lesson with some eavesdropping on the virtual mentors.

My friend Shirean is a songwriter. She went back to school as an adult to complete her degree in music and concocted something extraordinary for her senior project. Shirean invited *children* to participate in a live-performance guild. Young musicians, a visual artist, and a budding poet were given the opportunity to perform alongside seasoned musicians.

Shirean wove tales into the program to highlight the creative process that inspired each performance. Before singing "Picasso's Last Words," Shirean shared the back-story with the audience, I decided to do the same.

> *In 1973, the year that Picasso died, Dustin Hoffman and Paul McCartney dined together. McCartney recalls,*
>
> > *We were in Jamaica on holiday and we were staying in a little house outside Montego Bay, and we read in the local newspaper, The Daily Gleaner, that Dustin Hoffman and Steve McQueen were in town filming Papillion. They were just along the coast from us. We were saying it would be great to meet him, have dinner with him, so Linda rang up (Gambaccini).*
>
> *When Hoffman asked, Paul McCartney was able to explain how a song is made:*
>
> > *It's the same as you and acting; when the man says, 'Action!' you just pull it out of the bag, don't you? You don't know where it comes from, you just do it! How do you get all of your characterizations? It's just in you (Gambaccini).*

On their next meeting Hoffman challenged McCartney:

> *I've been thinking about this, I've seen a little thing in Time magazine about Picasso, and it struck me as being very poetic. I think this would be really great set to music (Gambaccini).*

McCartney took the challenge on the spot and responded to the creative impulse. As he sang Picasso's last words exactly as they were printed in Time, the actor exclaimed:

> *"Annie! Annie!" That's his wife. He says, "Annie! Annie! The most incredible thing! He's doing it! He's writing it! It's coming out!" He's leaping up and down, just like in the films, you know. And I'm knocked out because he's so appreciative (Gambaccini).*

But this is what I want you to remember. Later when Paul McCartney goes to record the song, "Picasso's Last Words," for the album, Band on the Run, he takes into account the article, the painter, and what he knows about cubism, and folds it all together.

McCartney recollects:

> *We thought we'd do this Picasso number, and we started off doing it straight. Then we thought, Picasso was kind of far out in his pictures, he'd done all these different kinds of things, fragmented. Cubism and the whole bit. I thought it would be*

> *nice to get a track a bit like that, put it through different moods, cut it up, edit it, mess around with it – like he used to do with his pictures. You see the old films of him painting; he paints it once and if he doesn't like it he paints it again, right on top of it, and by about twenty-five times he's got his picture. So we tried to use this kind of idea. I don't know much about it, to tell you the truth, but what we did know we tried to get in the song, sort of a Cubist thing (Gambaccini).*

Picasso was Paul McCartney's virtual mentor.

At this point in the storytelling, to hold the attention of my group of tweens and teens I launch into a speedy summary of Cubism:

> *Imagine you are a painter. Picasso basically decided on a subject matter, tore it to pieces, analyzed each part and then reassembled the subject on canvas, What results is something like this: Your mom was away and you break her favorite vase. Quickly you run to the junk drawer, heart pounding, for some Crazy Glue. You piece the vase back together, but it's never quite the same. Looking at a cubistic painting is like looking at an object through broken glass.*

They are tracking so I move on:

> *So we know that Picasso envisioned Cubism, yes, but Picasso, himself, was the first to admit that it was a painter named Paul Cezanne before him who forged the trail that he would choose to wander.*

> *As if I didn't know Cezanne! He was my one and only master! Don't you think I looked at his pictures? I spent years studying them... Cezanne! It was the same with all of us- he was our father. It was he who protected us (Ashton, 162).*

Cezanne was Picasso's virtual mentor.

Cubism's roots reach to the primitive art of Africa. Still, cubism is far from copycat. Picasso was learning from artists gone before him. An original work will always be birthed from the artist exploring a pocket of creative thought. The artist then carries what is discovered in that pocket forward and remolds it into something new.

If our creative voice is to emerge, if we are to make heads turn, the artist's impact must be loud. Cubism at the time of its conception was not only loud, but it was dissonant. Cubism jolted the art world into a modern era. Picasso's "Guernica" accomplished just that, and, in fact, its dissonance continues to elicit silence.

Eleven by twenty-five and a half feet of geometry, black and blue and white and grey; "Guernica" is Picasso's response to the art of war, his response to the bombing of the Basque town by the German Luftwaffe and the Italian Aviazone Legionaria during the Spanish Civil War. His canvas continues to remind humanity of the horrors of War.

Experiments with cubism would not be limited to

paint on canvas, as we saw in McCartney's song.

Fast forward, inspired by the images in Picasso's painting, poet Patti Smith was virtually mentored by "Guernica" and allowed it to inform her poem entitled, "The Geometry Blinked Ruin Unimaginable." A frequent visitor of Picasso's massive cubist canvas during the years it was protected in the Museum of Modern Art in New York City, her poem was penned when she paid a visit to her old friend "Guernica" in its rightful home, Madrid's Reina Sophia. She decided to translate the image to words.

Patti Smith's poem locks arms with Picasso's canvas in solidarity against the brutality of war. I imagine her on a street corner in NYC, pelting a crowd with images associated with the painting:

Horses wept jewels the size of fists
swept by scholars with a mind
to twist and level facets
of each plane to be raffled
when the bombing ceased

–The Geometry Blinked Ruin Unimaginable (excerpt), Patti Smith.

Patti Smith's poem challenges the viewer to contemplate different views of a grim reality–a Cubist poem.

Another artist captivated by "Guernica" is the granddaughter of Henri Matisse. Sophie Matisse transforms Picasso's painting to colors that seem to be straight from her grandfather's vivid palette. The result is a

> *bright reminder that Picasso's original statement is relevant in the 21st century. Sophie Matisse made a connection with her grandfather and his rival Picasso and, in so doing, raised her own creative voice.*

I suggest to my students that they are ready to gather from Picasso something of substance to incorporate into their own original work but first I give them one last charge from Picasso himself:

> *What do you think an artist is? An imbecile who only has eyes if he is a painter, or ears if he's a musician, or a lyre at every level of his heart if he's a poet, or even, if he's a boxer, just his muscle? ...NO, painting is not done to decorate apartments. It's an instrument of war for attack and defense against the enemy (Hensbergen 24).*

> *Picasso embraced his work, smashed the conventions of painting to shards and reassembled them in a way that geometrically amplified his voice.*

With their apprentice caps on, safely tucked inside our classroom guild, I had imparted the story, and explained to my students that it was their turn to converse with Picasso's canvas.

I challenged them to share their thoughts. Before digging in. Twelve-year-old Liam had this to say: "It's not *really* war but it means war. I think Picasso painted 'Guernica' to remind us that war is being mad at someone and expressing it through violence. It is a collection of depressed colors that express a sorrow we all can feel when we stop to look."

I knew we were ready to begin.

Directive

Do some further research of your own. Respond to Picasso's painting, "Guernica" with an original poem, a short story, visual work, or a musical composition.

Reflection

I am devoted to connecting students to pockets of creative collaboration, and encouraging them to participate. Cubism is a particular visual dialect that allows the artist to communicate in a specific way. Challenging students to communicate an original idea cubistically sheds light on the power of Cubism to elevate their voice. The following student work speaks volumes.

Picasso Imagining the Rose,

acrylic on wood assemblage

Eden, age 17

After "Guernica",
acrylic and ink
on canvas
Søren, age 8

kaleidoscopic night

Chrissy, age 15

Screams
pierce the musty air.

I'm running.

Running away from the agony
in my heart,

but I can't escape.

Shells rain down

from blackened sky.
Houses crackle
in smoky red.

Soot blinds me.
Sirens split the air.

I'm suffocating
in this fiery hell.

el esta por encima de las cenizas

Sharayah, 16

I hobble towards
what is left of this city
smothered in smoke,
this barren crater
dense with dust.

Flash of terrorizing
light, cymbal clash of glass,
I open my eyes as sky ash falls
on this rubble-garden
like snow on shock-stricken faces
staring through the big window

Mama and Papa
slouch, grimy fingers
kneading their bloodshot eyes.

There are no cobblestones
Echoing, no secrets shared
in the mystery of night,
only the wind and a fresh
flood of tears.

shadowing guernica

AJ, age 17

"Hey Sandy, hear anything about Mr. Wallace's criticism on my presentation?"

"No Mitchell." She replied.

"Okay," I said trying not to sound too disappointed. It's been five days since I showed him my new idea for the company and I could really use a raise. It would mean-

"Oh Mitchell, I nearly forgot. The new catalogue is ready for publishing. We just need you to sign it."

"Of course Sandy." As I walked back to her desk she handed me a pen and the form:

Sign here: *Mitchell Davis*

Date: *9/11/2001*

"Thank you," Sandy said in her gentle voice.

"Anytime," I replied.

Sitting in my ergonomic chair I blankly rolled # 2 pencils back and forth across my desk. The minutes felt like hours. It was still very early in the morning. Just as I began to nod off, my telephone rang. In the silence, it sounded like an air horn.

"Hello," I said in a groggy voice.

"Are you sleeping Mitchell? This is Mr. Wallace, come to my office immediately!"

As I gathered my thoughts, the dial tone brought me back to reality. Rising out of my chair I uneasily made my way towards Mr. Wallace's office. Before I knocked on his door his discomforting voice beckoned me in.

"Hello Mitchell," he greeted me with a wide smile.

"Hello Mr. Wallace," I said timidly. "You wanted to see me?"

"I sure did," he said, grinning even wider. "I wanted to talk to you about your presentation for the new winter line of clothing."

"Right," I said.

"You know Mitchell, I want you to know that what I am about to say to you I don't say to many people. In fact, this is only the third or fourth time I have said this to an employee in my life. Mitchell, you have vision. You remind me of a young version of myself. You-"

We fell to the floor as the building shook. Outside we could see nothing but a cloud of red smoke. After the explosion, all noise ceased. I saw Mr. Wallace waving at me, pointing to the door but I was glued to my spot, my body did not know what to do. Suddenly Mr. Wallace's mouth emitted sound.

"Move Mitchell! Let's go! The building across the street will collapse on us. We must evacuate at once."

My brain gained control over my movements again. We got out.

Once outside, rubble chased us. We tried to outrun it, but it was too quick. As the towers next door collapsed, so did our hope. The world as we knew it disappeared. The plaster dust storm swallowed us whole, leaving nothing but scrapes for the hardened firefighters.

Before we were devoured by the rubble Mr. Wallace said something peculiar to me waving his hands in the air: "Mitchell, this is our 'Guernica'."

Tolkien's Allegorical Leaf

Concept and Objectives

Introduce middle and high school aged apprentices to the creative process of author J.R.R Tolkien. Explore Tolkien's short story, "Leaf by Niggle" and mine for gold.

- Promote critical creative thinking in the area of literary analysis
- Stimulate the creative impulse
- Explore the steps involved in the writing process
- Craft an original critical essay in response to a short story

Required Materials

- "Leaf by Niggle," by J.R.R. Tolkien
- "Paper and pencil for note taking

Possible Connections To Other Subjects

Following are suggestions for further research:

- Explore allegorical works as John Bunyan's *Pilgrim's Progress*, George Orwell's *Animal Farm* or Edmund Spenser's, *The Faerie Queen.*
- Explore allegory in visual arts and the literal meaning of what is depicted. The work of artists ranging from Thomas Cole and his series, *The Course of Empire*, to contemporary artist, Jasper Johns and his iconic images are worth consideration.

Back Story, Lesson, and Charge

> *Now that we've read, "Leaf by Niggle," let's begin with a little background on the author. I suppose I got carried away listening to my own words:*
>
> *...here is a man who endured his share of tragedy— he and his brother were orphaned as children... a man who helped bring shape to the Oxford English Dictionary— in charge of all the words with a Germanic origin from the letter W forward... here is a self-proclaimed procrastinator submitting a manuscript to his publisher that contained over half a million words and stood in a stack seven feet high from what I hear...*

I wanted to mention Tolkien's work at Leeds, his professorship at Merton College, Oxford, wanted to introduce his take on *Beowulf*, but instead bit my tongue. I decided to save something for next year.

I began this particular lesson with an offering:

> *Here is what I know of how Tolkien crafted 'Leaf by Niggle:*
>
> *...do you realize that Tolkien communicated that he wrote this story with ease? Basically he incubated the idea in his mind and was able to capture it on the page in one fell swoop.*

I saw a few eyes bulge. After many months engaging in the process of bringing an idea to the page, I had no doubt they knew exactly what he meant. These are students who understand that writing is a process that usually involves extensive revision. Still, I had to ask, *"How could Tolkien accomplish this?"*

There were a few passive shrugs, but I was pleased that the majority of these students recognized that Tolkien was able to translate his imagination to paper because he had established a writing discipline.

Directive

Write a critical essay of J.R.R. Tolkien's "Leaf by Niggle." Be sure to include summary, commentary, and personal reflection.

Reflection

Tolkien was responding to his creative impulse. He was willing to engage in the work of shaping his idea. I sat back and watched our virtual mentor challenge my students to engage in the chaos of an idea taking shape, to press into their individual genius. I reveled, watching the gears mesh.

No two fingerprints are alike. Every author has a distinct writing style. *Voice* is the fingerprint of an author. Reading through this last stack of essays for the year I knew the required assignment had done more than earn each of my students an A+.

These culminating essays proved to me that these individuals are beginning to grasp the power of words. These are students whose curiosity prompts them to dig into the work of harnessing an original idea. Following are excerpts from our pre-writing discussion:

> *"Niggle is a silly little man who loves to paint. He isn't very good at it, but that's because he always gets distracted."*

"...a small man with an irritatingly kind heart that distracts him from his life's work: a huge painting of a tree."

"In a world with strict laws, lives Niggle who is especially fond of his most recent endeavor... but he never can seem to find enough time for working."

"Because of Niggle I am considering the major lesson of treating others how I want to be treated in my life. Whether it's buying someone lunch, giving someone a ride to school, or just being a friend, I want to be a giving person who treats others with respect. Life is so short, it would be a waste of time to spend it all on myself."

"This short story is Tolkien's way of saying "We all need to step up, work hard, and do everything to avoid laziness."

"I too am lazy. Unfortunately, laziness has become a habit that is very hard to break away from. For me, being lazy means sitting on the couch, watching my favorite TV show while eating a scrumptious bowl of something instead of doing homework. Laziness is curling up on my bed listening to my iPod, while I close my eyes and doze off instead of doing my chores. Being diligent is a skill that I need to practice. It may take some time out of my everyday like working out for a marathon. I can't just sit on the couch eating potato chips and then expect to run a 26-mile race. I have to condition and workout everyday to build up the stamina and strength to win that marathon!"

"The story has motivated me with the details and circumstances it uses to unveil truths about the characters and life. I fantasize about using those techniques in my own writing. I have thought long and hard about the themes described in this book."

"This is basically a short story about a physically small man who thinks on a larger scale. Sometimes his need for perfection leads to procrastination."

"Laziness is not a thing to be tampered with because sometimes the mischievous creature can weave itself into your heart."

"Tolkien's passion bleeds out of the pages and drips on your hands but you can't really feel it until it flows through your heart."

"What else would you expect from a man who edited the last four letters of the Oxford English Dictionary?"

The Poetry of Words

Concept and Objectives

- Introduce 3rd grade through high school aged apprentices to the value of specificity in poetry and the connections between words and images.
- Spark the creative impulse

- Promote critical creative thinking in the area of creative writing and visual arts
- Explore the steps involved in the creative process
- Craft a visual collage poem

Required Materials

- A stack of dictionaries
- Magazines
- Scissors
- Glue sticks
- White paint, brushes, water
- Chalk pastel
- Glitter
- Construction paper
- Dymo Label Maker and tape

Possible Connections To Other Subjects

Following are suggestions for further research:

- Sestinas, when crafted well, have a collage effect. Read Elizabeth Bishop's famous poem entitled, "Sestina" online. Because the writer is limited by the end words, specificity is vital and the resulting poem will become an interesting collage of sound and rhythm. A sestina is a seven-stanza poem, with six lines per stanza, except stanza 6, which has only three lines. Six words that are introduced in stanza one are rotated in a specific pattern at the end of each line throughout the poem.

The pattern works as follows:

1 2 3 4 5 6	End words of lines in stanza 1
6 1 5 2 4 3	End words of lines in stanza 2
3 6 4 1 2 5	End words of lines in stanza 3
5 3 2 6 1 4	End words of lines in stanza 4
4 5 1 3 6 2	End words of lines in stanza 5
2 4 6 5 3 1	End words of lines in stanza 6
(6 2) (1 4) (5 3)	Middle and end words of stanza 7

Following are some examples from my classroom guild:

sally of the sea

Jonathan, age 12

Her reflection bounces as she **glides**,
toes skimming the endless plane of sea. **Sally**
twirls and twist, her baby blue dress **billowing**.
Chestnut hair snakes upon the **brackish**
water and slaps the choppy **sea**.
A northeasterly tempts her to **dive**

into his grasp, the imprudent **dive**
will end her reckless **gliding**,
Her image angers the **brackish**
eyes that want her airborne talents. **Sally**
avoids the chilly, icy grasp of the **sea**,
but this of lack of familiarity **billows**

around to see the fist of a wave **billow**
her iridescent legs as she starts her **dive**,
plunging into shock by the **brackish**
glee of the ocean. No longer **gliding**,
vulnerable to the playful plan that **Sally**
had for so long denied the **sea**.

Unforgiving, the ravenous **sea**
tosses her, ebb and flow, as trusses **billow**
around her blanched body. **Sally**
is forced into another perilous **dive**
her days of youthful **gliding**
over the old and bent **brackish**

stare of the **brackish**
malevolence of the churning **sea**.
The snickering seaweed **glides**
Across her face, tangles and **billows**
without mercy. Firmly **diving**
their prickly tentacles into **Sally's**

soft skin. Gasping for breath **Sally**
flails up through the undulation of **brackish**
eyes. Her enemy unscrolls, **diving**
into her heart with vengeance only the **sea**
can muster. A man, blue as Poseiden's eyes **billows**
out, glowering triumphantly he **glides**

above Sally. He lifts a wavering arm and **dives**
his slivery hand into brackish memories, **gliding**
above billowing hair. The sea grants Sally no **clemency**.

live vicariously, die vicariously

inspired by Degas

Evelyn, age 17

On a rigid wooden bench the black **widow**
stares at the ground, shunning her **ballerina**.
One twirling pirouette caused the dancer's **foot**
and future to fracture in splintering **seconds**.
Broken, she buries her face in **tulle**.
Closing her eyes, she avoids the widow's **silence**.

With her memories screaming, **silence**
proves too loud. Once the **widow**
too, glided across dance floors, **tulle**
bouncing. She was the **ballerina**.
The years escaped in **seconds**.
Injury befell her ribbon-laced **foot**.

Worn hardwood **underfoot**,
the ballerina danced in **silence**.
Her reflection morphed within **seconds**.
Humiliated by the fumble, the black **widow**
blinks to erase the image of her **ballerina**
crumpled on the ground in disheveled **tulle**.

A fouetté jeté then pirouette in **tulle**
shattered her satin clad **foot**.
Flung to the floor, the petite **ballerina**
shrieked in pain, piercing the **silence**.
To her side rushed a begrudging **widow**.
Two dreams destroyed in **seconds**.

Paralyzed, tick tick tick passing **seconds**,
the ballerina studies her torn **tulle**,
avoiding the gaze of the black **widow**.
The widow whose aching **foot**
wallows in disappointment, whoe **silence**
spawns frustration with her **ballerina**.

This can't be the end, muses the **ballerina**.
She grasps at hope, whiling away **seconds**
before the doctor can disturb the **silence**.
Sneaking a glance at the tattered **tulle**
the black widow scowls. Never did my **foot**
recover and nor shall hers, prophesies the **widow**.

Ornate tulle will never veil a withered **foot**,
Prior seconds can't be re-wound. The **widow**
and her pale ballerina sit disillusioned in **silence**

- Explore collage in visual arts and the impact of mixed media on what is depicted. Synthetic Cubism, photomontage, the decoupage works of Henri Matisse, are worth exploring. In visual collage, specificity of the pastiche of image is vital.

Back Story, Lesson, and Charge

Words.

Writing begins with words.

Enacting poetry is a great way to get excited about words.

Rainy days were bittersweet when I was in elementary school. While the playground was sorely missed, watching the rain run like a waterfall down the side of our classroom made of glass was poetic. And of course, there were the rainy day games to brighten the atmosphere. I remember one teacher in particular who introduced us to the best rainy day game of all: Dictionary. She would choose a word that none of us had ever heard and then have us write our made-up definition for the word on a slip of paper. We dropped the definitions into a basket, then she randomly read them out loud and we voted for our favorite. When she read the real definition from the dictionary, she planted, seed by seed, an appreciation for words that has not left me these many years later.

Once, while teaching poetry on a rainy day, I remembered that teacher and the classroom with the glass wall, and with a dictionary in hand, began my own lesson. We were reading a poem by William Wordsworth, and I began by having my students think of the poet's last name as a really great compound word. I went on to share my rainy day memory and began exploring vocabulary from "Composed Upon Westminster Bridge, September 3, 1802," Wordsworth's famous sonnet.

We were about to embark on a game of Dictionary with a twist. I would attempt to take my students on a field trip across that bridge, enable them to compose their very own poem. When I gave them the first word to tackle, their definitions were non-specific, close to the real thing, but not precise. I opened the dictionary, flipped then ran my finger down a page, "*Infuse*, to fill; pervade." I read the second definition, "To release flavor or healing properties while being soaked," and then I infused tea in a glass mug of steaming water. The students liked this so much that we began experimenting. We infused darkness with light by closing blinds and watching light stream in through the slits. We lit candles in dark corners. We watched color bleed onto wet watercolor paper.

We spent some time *steeping* ourselves in words.

After our little game of Dictionary we took a few steps across the bridge, time for the real lesson to begin. I had them close their eyes and *steep* themselves, in Wordsworth's poem, encouraged them to let words seep into their ears,

> *The sounds of words matter, so does the shape.*

Now the students in my workshop were curious,

> *Shape?*

> *Yes, shape.*

Writers of all ages often forget the vital connection between words and image.

I led them into another room, to a table laden with jars of glitter, paint and brushes, drawing pencils, chalk pastels, scissors, glue sticks, stacks of newspaper and magazines, and a basket of Dymo label makers. It was time for my students to "find" poetry and in the process discover the power of words.

I showed the students how to begin with a random block,

> *Rip out several paragraphs or blocks of words from a page of newspaper or magazine.*

I instructed them to read the block of words outside the context of the article,

> *Now the poet must think about the specific meaning of the words being read and imagine a new, personalized context to place the block of words into.*

I showed them how to block out certain words to make their new context emerge and to become an original poem.

Directive

Once I set them free to explore the supplies on the table, they didn't need much instruction beyond, "Create a poetic collage."

Reflection

I am devoted to connecting writers to words by teaching them to crave what all good writers crave: *Specificity*.

Taking time to consider words is an undervalued skill, is often considered a tedious task. But words are audacious.

Taking the "boring" out of something ultimately involves changing the attitude about the task. Exploring words is an adventure. Learning to use a dictionary—the kind that you hold in your hands—is a skill that over time will allow young writers to infuse the worth of words into the world.

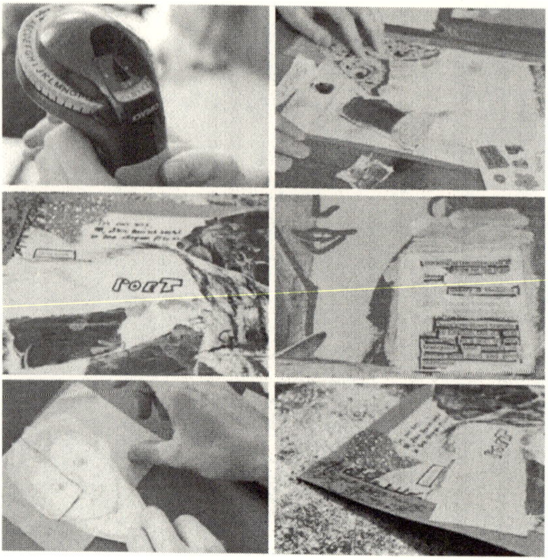

Discovering Genius Between the Folds

Concept and Objectives

"All our knowledge has its origins in our perceptions."

-Leonardo da Vinci

Too often educators segment academic disciplines into neat little boxes. Creative thinkers like Leonardo are able to seamlessly and simultaneously meander science and art. The goal of this lesson is to demonstrate the intersection of science and the arts. This is a fun lesson for elementary, middle and high school aged apprentices.

- Spark the creative impulse
- Promote critical creative thinking in the area of science and visual arts
- Explore the steps involved in the creative process
- Explore the design, function, and potential of mitochondria
- Fold a hyperbolic parabola

Required Materials

- Diagram of mitochondria
- How to: Origami Hyperbolic Parabola *(search the internet for instructions and videos, also called a "saddle")*
- Paper, pre-cut according to instructions above
- DVD, *Between the Folds*

Possible Connections To Other Subjects

Following are suggestions to explore:

- Explore origami and its connection to math. *Project Origami,* by Thomas Hull is an excellent resource and a good place to begin.
- Create a collage or visual montage of the cell. Explore the origin of scientific terms, such as "mitochondria" and discover the value of language specificity. Research the function of the cell organelles as metaphor and create a poem or short allegory to accompany the visual work.

Back Story, Lesson, and Charge

There are several words that sang above the rest in my high school science classes.

From botany, photosynthesis is the one.

From marine biology, Echinodermata and Coelenterata.

From chemistry, stoichiometry.

And, from cellular biology, mitochondria captured my imagination."

So begins the lesson.

Mitochondria located in the cytoplasm are little energy factories within the cell. These amazing organelles enable respiration, which allows the cell to move, to divide, and to insure each cell's unique purpose.

Mitochondria can have different shapes depending on the cell type. Because they contain their own DNA, ribosomes, and can produce their own protein, mitochondria are only partially dependant upon the host cell.

What I set out to explore with my students is the fact that mitochondria possess a double membrane, an outer, which is smooth, and an inner, which possesses many folds called cristae which exponentially increase membrane surface area.

All living cells have mitochondria. But it is amazing to consider that typical animal cells have up to 2000 mitochondria... in each cell!

I wanted to take their imagination on a journey between these folds.

Folds give mitochondria their unique potential; enable the organelle to be highly productive. Cristae take batches of sugar and oxygen and produce ATP (adenosine triphosphate)—cell food.

At the beginning of the year, science began by exploring the idea that science and art are uniquely connected. Leonardo himself reminds us, "All our knowledge has its origins in our perceptions."

My hope was to connect the exploration of mitochondria to the unit we had just completed on the human nervous system. We explored the potential of individuality as we explored the brain—human potential, genius. And here another potential to bridge the gap between learning information and sparking individuality presented itself, this time on a cellular level.

So today, to continue our exploration of mitochondria, we are going to watch a film about origami.

Yes, origami.

I then provided instructions and large pre-cut squares of paper for the students to fold a hyperbolic parabola. We did this to reinforce the film's message that even paper has hidden potential.

Folding paper is work. But folding is important work. Your work will utilize a fraction of this sheet of the

> *paper's potential. Remember, the paper you hold in your hands will never be the same.*

Dare I say, neither will they?

I think *mitochondria* is one of those words that will stick.

Directive

Follow the origami instructions and fold a hyperbolic parabola.

Reflection

The students gathered around the TV.I popped in the DVD and set out to accomplish some administrative goals.

Not far into the film I overheard the little group letting out sighs of amazement. I was pleased. I witnessed something that surprised me. One-by-one, individual students from the group of 5th through 11th graders got up to grab a handful of paper and began folding.

They were folding.

The film did not provide a directive for viewers to participate. This was not a fold-along film. These students were engaging in this work spontaneously.

Being inspired is a magnificent rush.

bibliography

Arcade Fire, The. "Wake Up." *Funeral.* Durham: Merge Records, 2004.

Ashton, Dore, ed. *Picasso On Art.* New York: De Capo Press, 1972.

Assayas, Michka. *Bono in Conversation with Michka Assayas.* New York: Penguin Publishing Group, 2005.

Buechner, Frederick. *Telling the Truth: The Gospel as Tragedy, Comedy, & Fairy Tale.* San Francisco: Harper San Francisco, 1977.

Bayles, David and Orland, Ted. *Art and Fear: Observations On The Perils (and Rewards) of Artmaking.* Eugene: Image Continuum Press, 2007.

Baxter, Charles. *Through the Safety Net.* New York: Vintage Books, 1998.

Caroll, Lewis. *Alice's Advetures in Wonderland and Through the Lokking Glass.* New York: Penguin, 2000.

Cole, Bruce. *The Renaissance Artist at Work: From Pisano to Titian.* Boulder: Westview Press, 1990.

Cowling, Elizabeth, et al. *Matisse Picasso.* New York: Tate Publishing, 2002.

Elie, Paul. *The Life You Save May be Your Own: An American Pilgrimage.* New York: Farrar, Straus and Giroux, 2004.

Frost, Robert. The Road Not Taken: A Selection. New York: Henry Holt and Company, 1971.

Gambaccini, Paul. "The Rolling Stone Interview: Paul McCartney." The Rolling Stone, 31 January 1974.

Gatto, John. *Dumbing Us Down.* Gabriola Island: New Society, 2002.

Healy, Melissa. "Beyond the Mozart Effect." The Los Angeles Times, 1 March 2010: E1 +. Print.

Hensbergen, Gijs Van. *Guernica: Biography of a Twentieth Century Icon*. New York: Blomsbury Publishing, 2004.

Johnson, Paul. *Creators*. New York: HarperCollins Publishers, 2006.

Kasabian. "Where Did All the Love Go?" *West Ryder Pauper Lunatic Asylum*. New York: Red Int / Red Ink, 2009.

Legge, James. *Confucian Analects*. Whitefish: Kessinger Publishing, LLC, 2004.

L'Engle, Medeleine. *Walking on Water: Reflections on Faith and Art*. Wheaton: Harold Shaw Publishers, 1980.

Lionni, Leo. *Frederick*. New York: Scholastic, Inc. 1967.

Makarova, Elena. *Friedl Dicker-Brandeis 1898 – 1944*. Jewish Women's Archive. http://jwa.org/encyclopedia/article/dicker-brandeis-friedl

Morgan, Genevieve. Matisse: *The Artist Speaks*. San Francisco: Collins Publishers, 1996.

Mumford and Sons. "The Cave." *Sigh No More*. New York: Glassnote Records, 2010.

O'Connor, Flannery. *Everything that Rises Must Converge*. New York: Farrar, Straus, Giroux, 1956.

Paris, K.. *A leadership model for planning and implementing change for school-to-work transition*. Madison: University of Wisconsin-Madison, Center on Education and Work, 1994.

Polacco, Patricia. *Appelemando's Dreams*. New York: Putnam Juvenile, 1997.

Prager, Dennis. *Happiness is a Serious Problem*. New York: Harper's Collins Publishers, 1998.

Radiohead. "2+2=5." *Hail to the Thief*. Los Angeles: Capital, 2003.

Robinson, Ken. *Out of our Minds: Learning to be Creative.* West Sussex: Capstone Publishing Limited, 2001.

Robinson, Ken. *The Element: How Finding Your Passion Changes Everything.* New York: Viking, 2009.

Salamon, Judy. "Keeping Creativity Alive." New York Times, September 10, 2004. http://www.nytimes.com/2004/09/10/arts/design/10SALA.html

Smith, Patti. *Auguries of Innocence.* New York: CCCO, an imprint of Harpers Collins Publishers, 2005.

Van Gogh, Vincent. *The Complete Letters of Vincent Van Gogh with Reproductions of All the Drawings in Correspondence.* New York: New York Graphic Society, 1959.

Van Gogh, Vincent. *The Letters of Vincent Van Gogh.* New York: Penguin Group, 1997.

Varga, George. "U2 Opener Uneven Yet Uplifting, Unifying," The Sandego Union Tribune, March 30, 2005: http://www.signonsandiego.com/uniontrib/20050330/news_1c30u2.html.

Virginia Euwer Wolff. *The Mozart Season.* New York: Square Fish, 2007.

Volavkova, Hanna, editor. *I Never Saw Another Butterfly: Children's Drawings and Poems from Terezin Concentration Camp, 1942-1944.* New York: Schocken Books, 1993.

Williams, Nathan. "Take on the World." *King of the Beach.* Oxford: Fat Possum, 2010.

Williams, Tennessee. *The Theatre of Tennessee Williams, Volume 1.* New York: New Directions Books, 1971.

Wilson, David Mackay. "Developmentally Appropriate Practice in the Age of Testing." Harvard Education Letter, 25.3 (2009): Web. March 11, 2011.